Being Single Is A Ministry

Casey Jackson-Ware

Casey Jackson–Ware

About The Author

Casey Jackson Ware was born and raised in a traditional household in Greenwood, Mississippi. After a successful nine year career within the financial sector, Casey has made the step toward being an Indie author, in hopes of spiritually uplifting readers experiencing internal struggles. Her goal is to influence her audience into being self-reflective and self-corrective individuals. Casey now lives in Minnesota, where she enjoys the winter weather with her husband and teenage son.

When she's not lending her expertise as a financial manager or journaling for writing projects, she's serving as First Lady for the True Foundation Church Of God In Christ alongside her husband, Senior Pastor, Elder Dion Merlyn Ware. She's committed to orchestrating outreach within the local community.

Being Single Is A Ministry is her debut as a self-published author, meant to reach individuals that may be wrestling with their single lifestyle and the pressure, insecurities and despairs that comes with it.

Casey Jackson–Ware

Dedication

I would like to dedicate this book to my spiritual father the late Superintendent Apostle Dr. Kurtiz F. Boudoir, Founder of Book of Acts Church International, RMI.

Acknowledgments

I would like to first thank my Creator, my Savior, my God. I thank God for his grace, mercy, and his long suffering. I am so grateful that God did not give up on me. I thank God for his spirit leading and guiding me in this book. He spoke and He allowed me to write. I'm grateful for the leading of the Holy Spirit.

My son, Je'Kylon "JJ" Jackson, I thank God for you being my motivation. You have inspired me to change my life and to live Holy before God so that you can see that we have to trust in the Lord for all things.

My sister, Natasha (Jackson) Hollowell, I appreciate you for taking the time to read my book every time I wrote a chapter. You were my first reader. Though you aren't a big reader, you never complained about the amount of material I brought to you. To my parents, Ada & Willie Jackson, thank you for believing in me, encouraging and relentlessly motivating me to succeed in life.

I would like to thank my former Pastor the late Apostle, Kurtiz F. Boudoir, for the Bible teachings and teaching me how to fall in love with Christ for myself. I appreciate every rebuke and correction. He spoke into my life about this masterpiece. He told me to "write the book and make it plain". He had a chance to read the first few chapters in this book before he went to sleep in the Lord and he encouraged me to complete it. I miss him dearly. I know that he would be Godly proud of me. I appreciate his wife as well Evangelist Grace Boudoir. She taught me how to carry myself as a Godly woman and how to prepare myself for my spouse.

To my best friend, Treka (White) House, you are absolutely remarkable. I had given up on publishing my book, but you pushed me, you kept me informed, and put me in contact with different individuals that could help me move forward. You have always believed in me and nudged me towards greatness. Thanks for the late night chats and for always being there for me, no matter what you had going on in your life.

Hats off to my book designer, Gabriel Wallace, you are better than fantastic. You were patient and very knowledgeable. I reached out to you on Facebook after reading your book "Book of Revelations," which is a very profound and an excellent read. I told you my vision and you designed my book cover exactly as I envisioned it. Amazing job Gabe!

To my editor, Lashunda (Foreman) Claiborn, thanks for your willingness to edit my book in the middle of writing your Dissertation. You did not hesitate when I asked for your help. In fact, you were so eager to do so. Thank you isn't nearly enough!

I thank God for every man that was a part of my life the good, the bad, and the ugly. I learned what I did not want in a husband. I learned what to accept and what not to accept. I learned not to settle. They taught me how to pray and wait on God.

Last but not least my Boaz, Dion Ware. Thanks for answering the call of God. Thanks for believing in me and encouraging me. Thanks for supporting my many many aspirations. I'm grateful for you. I'm grateful that I waited on God to bring you to me. "Whosoever finds a wife finds a good thing, and obtains favor of the LORD." Proverbs 18:22

Dear Readers,

I want to start by thanking you for purchasing "Being Single Is A Ministry". This book was written when I was single and yearning for a mate, a God-given mate. I was in a place where I didn't desire the desperation of rushed relationships that weren't ordained to be mine. I had already been there and done that. I wanted a blessed marriage sent from heaven. I was in the process of understanding my worth as well as learning patience with a destiny I couldn't foresee. I am now a married woman of God. My life has not been perfect and I want you all to see the mistakes that I've made in search of a husband. The most valuable lesson I learned during that time, was not to actually search for anyone, but to sit still to be found. Just because I'm saved and I'm a First Lady, doesn't mean I am or will ever be a woman of perfection. I don't aim to please man, but my Father in heaven; for my trials and tribulations are seeds sown for my purpose. My past faults shaped me into being a profound woman, which sculptured me for my role as First Lady. I am first a human, which means I'm flawed and second a woman, meaning I was designed with specific desires to be connected to a mate in purpose. I want women all around me to understand that life, love and relationships all require experience and a process, none of which includes perfection. Everything starts with self. I have no desire to wear a mask, but instead to lend my experiences to aid in the growth in as many women as possible. My faith and beliefs made this book possible. I want each person reading this to understand that you are worthy, your life was designed to be your own and you will never walk the same road as someone else. Please use my history has guidance and as a chance to self-reflect over who you are. Don't be chained by judgment or allow your path to be sidetracked by unproductive opinions and unnecessary ridicule, prepare yourselves from the inside for your future. No one can love and appreciate you, until you're able to do it for yourself. Thank you so much again for supporting my movement to aid in the improvement of self-love amongst women. I pray that you all thoroughly enjoy this book and that it encourages you to change yourself, before you enter your next relationship.

Love Always,

Casey Jackson-Ware

Interview with Casey Jackson-Ware on Being Single

But seek ye first the kingdom of God, and his righteousness; and all these things shall be added unto you. Matthew 6:33

When you are from a small town in Mississippi, your dreams of a limitless life aren't necessarily on the top of the teacher's lesson plans. Many of our parents are simply trying to keep us alive, get us through high school and quickly push us into independent adults. Going to college and establishing an actual career is simply a bonus. As we journey about our life, however we decide to do so, we soon learn that path that we mentally paved for ourselves was modified by something that held more value; being of service to someone else. Being from a small town, sometimes reduces our dreams to be small ones, but there are so many that dispute the fact that it has to be that way. Deriving from a smaller community has it benefits, as it gives us more intimate connections and room to grow. I would know, I'm from Greenwood, Mississippi; a town barely spotted on a map. I know so many talented, intellectual and successful individuals from my small town and Casey Jackson-Ware happens to be one of them. Casey is a product of a traditional, working class family from Mississippi. She now has a family of her own and she wears many hats, including her latest, author. Today is a special day for Casey Jackson-Ware as she releases her debut as an author, Being Single Is A Ministry. Being Single Is A Ministry is currently available for purchase, get your copy today by clicking here. This book will change the life of so many single women; don't miss your opportunity for a personal transformation.

Casey is a native of Greenwood, Mississippi, where she graduated from Greenwood High School in 1999. She later graduated with her Bachelor of Science in Business Administration with an emphasis in Management from the University of Memphis and National American University with her MBA. She has had a successful presence and influence in the financial sector for the last nine years, where she thrives; however, spiritual inspiration is where she finds her greatest joy. I could go on and on about Casey, but it wouldn't be an interview if she didn't speak.

Casey, let's open up your interview with something

transparent you want the readers to know about you.

Casey: Many people view me as strong, courageous, intelligent, willful, educated and independent. At one point in my life, I lacked the confidence that those words represented, and I knew they didn't apply to me. Based on my life experiences, I can now own those words as a realistic part of my character. They now define me. I have been in the shoes of single women. I have worn the shoes of a scoured woman. I have owned the shoes of a woman that lacks self-worth. I have modeled in the shoes of a woman wanting and desiring the comfort of a man. I have sported the shoes where I look for others to define who I am. I have been in a place where I have lost myself in a relationship that didn't even take me a mile upward. I have been hurt, abused, and most of all; I was a scarred woman who has been healed by the blood of Jesus. That is my truth, I own it and I live it.

What's the name of your book and tell us why you chose that name?

Casey: The name of my book is Being Single Is A Ministry. This is the title the Lord gave me as I was journaling. He constantly reminded me that the position I was in was a ministering position.

Tell us what your book is about.

Casey: Being Single Is A Ministry is a book that is intended to speak to the mind, body, and soul of single women. It is a book that will encourage those with low self-esteem, those that lack self-confidence. This book will help women to fall in love with themselves, enhance their relationship with Christ, and prepare themselves for the man that God has preordained for them.

Exactly what was going on in your life that made you decide to write a book?

Casey: I was in a ministry where the Pastor was strict and preached Holiness or Hell. He would always say, "There is no such thing as a boyfriend or girlfriend when you are in Christ". Well, I was in a relationship and I was trying my best to hold on to it. It wasn't that I really wanted the relationship but I didn't want to be alone. When God begin to convict me, I knew that I needed to let some things and people go. I learned that I can't take everyone on the journey God has for me. So I begin to deal with myself. My outlet has always been writing; so I begin to journal my thoughts, my actions, my emotions and my day to day activity. I was writing everything down. I go back now and read some of things that I've written and I just smile at my growth.

What did you learn about yourself as you drafted what is now your finished product?

Casey: I learned that I had very low self-esteem. I was a people pleaser first. I knew that I had the capability to succeed in all areas of life but I let others pull me down with their thoughts and opinions of me.

Think about the most challenging part of being single for you. If you could go back in time and tell the single Casey anything, what would it be? Why?

Casey: My most challenging moment while I was single was watching my son have to deal with issues of not having a stable man in his life. I felt like I needed to settle just so he could have someone he could call dad. I would tell myself again today, "Wait on the Lord"

What role did your faith play as your mind transformed as a single woman?

Casey: My faith in God played a major role in my transformation. Jesus is my life; I wouldn't have a testimony if it wasn't for Him. It wasn't until I accepted Christ as my personal savior that I realized it was me all along. I was the one with the self-esteem problems, the insecurities, the lack of value and hope for myself, not the men I was in the relationship with. So when the Lord began to reveal myself to me, I knew that a transformation needed to take place.

What changes did you make in how you conducted yourself in your single status?

Casey: One way I begin to conduct myself as a single was to value my body. I learned that my body was a temple of GOD and first and foremost I needed to keep it sacred. I called it "secondary virginity," I begin to practice abstinence; I became celibate until marriage. I decided to stop given up my most prize possession. It wasn't always easy. In those hard times, I found myself praying and praying and praying harder until the feeling and desire would subside.

How was your self-esteem impacted as a single woman? Has it changed? Was marriage the reason for change? If not, what was?

Casey: I believe my self-esteem was impacted long before becoming a single woman. I think it was shattered when I was a little girl by society and people. Because of this, I stepped in and out of relationships, broken and looking for someone to put me back together. My self-esteem has changed. It wasn't an overnight process, it actually took years and there are some things I am still working on. Now I have confidence in who I am, because of Christ. I have learned not to define myself by the appearances, material things, talents, and success of others. I measure myself by the word of God. I am fearfully and wonderfully made. So I love every curve and inch of myself I love my accomplishments and my mistakes. Although I desired to be married, marriage wasn't my reason for change. I am the reason for change. Once God did a self-examination on me, I didn't like the person he had shown me. So I had to do some self-adjustments for myself.

If you would have known as a single woman what you now know as a married woman, what difference do you think it would have made?

Casey: It would have made a lot of difference. I would have first saved my most prized possession for my husband. I wouldn't have allowed people to change who I was.

Facing our past and touching our pain puts us in a vulnerable state, so often times we don't. We simply move on and hope we leave all the ugliness behind, but sometimes it's not so easy. **Do you think what you experienced being single affected you as married woman now? If so, how?**

Casey: Of course! There are times in my marriage now where I have to step back and say, "Casey, this is your husband, not a fling, not your boyfriend; but this is your life partner -- until death do us part." I learned a lot about myself while I was single, some of which have served a great purpose in our marriage. Other life occurrences sometimes cause me to put up walls when I shouldn't.

As you look back, what positive lessons did you take from your single experience?

Casey: The most positive lesson I have learned from my single experience, is that I had to fall in love with God first and from there, he taught me how to love myself.

There are so many women wanting a husband, some are even desperate. What advice would you give these women?

Casey: Wait on God. Proverb 18:22, "Whoso find a wife find a good thing, and obtain favor of the Lord"···. Women stop searching and let the man find you. That is his job not yours. Hide yourself in Christ. During this time seek ye first the kingdom of God and wait patiently on the Lord to add to your life. Take this time and fall in love with yourself.

What are your hopes for your book?

Casey: My hope is that single (unmarried) women will begin to value themselves and stop falling for what's given versus what you deserve. My wish is that they will allow God to mold them, heal them, rebuild them, and restore them from their brokenness; making them whole in preparation for the predestined Boaz God has for them.

You have the floor. What do you want to say to those

reading your interview?

Casey: I want to encourage my readers to take a moment and evaluate yourself. If you have been waiting, hoping in and out of relationship or wishing that the right one would appear, I want to encourage you to embrace your single lifestyle. God put us in different situations and life experiences for a reason. Take this time to love who God has made you to be. Make improvement for God and yourself. Stop hiding behind the mask that you think other people want to see and be yourself. Define who you are as a single woman, so you won't get lost as a married woman.

This day is extremely exciting for me, since Casey Jackson—Ware is my best friend. As we cross the finish—line to our dreams, we all are hopeful that we have the support of those we love, waiting for us. Well, I have my pom poms pumping in the air and I'm cheering from California to Minnesota for my friend. Casey has been present for every great milestone in my life. She has not missed one opportunity to be an extraordinary friend to me. She has encouraged me every step of the way and supported me mentally, spiritually, emotionally and even financially during our twenty year friendship. Words cannot express how much she means to me, so to say that I'm completely overjoyed to be the first one to interview her, is definitely an understatement. We all only dream to have everlasting, rare friendships; especially with individuals who want nothing but the best for us. I'm very fortunate to have been one to capture that rarity. Well, let me stop right now, because my emotions are rising. I can't help it, I'm a water sign. Nevertheless, I'm having a proud moment for my friend, because I know how much she has anticipated this day. What a blessing it is! Congratulations Casey!

Please enjoy your copy of <u>Being Single Is A Ministry</u>. I pray that you find the guidance and encouragement God intended as necessary to the best single you possible.

This interview can be found at <u>www.trekahouse.com</u> under the <u>Blog</u> tab. Please be sure to check out this site for more inspirational and interesting topics. Additionally, <u>Breaking Point</u>, an extraordinary fiction book written by my best friend, Treka L. House can be purchased there.

Content

Preface

Being Single is a Ministry, a manuscript that came from a journal of God's words to me when I was in a transitioning period from being in a relationship to being single. As I began to reread my journal and I recognized the growth, I knew this was not only for me but to help others as well. This book is intended to reach women who suffer with low self-esteem, those that seek validation from a man, those that are looking for love in all the wrong places, and those that have allowed a relationship to take precedence over God. Being single is not just for those that aren't in a relationship but it is for those that aren't married, but have a boyfriend, boo, friend with benefits, side kick, shacking partner, and the likes. This manuscript is meant to bring clarity, which allows you to view your current position as a ministry and value yourself because you are God's most prized possession. This moment in your life is designed to draw you closer to our Lord and Savior. It is also an opportunity to get to know yourself.

I wanted to put myself in this book; my testimony, and how I overcame. God allowed me to go through different situations to draw me closer to him. I waited on God and allowed him to do the work. My self-esteem has been restored. My self-value has been increased. I now find my validation in Jesus Christ based on what he has already promised me. I have learned to wait on the Lord in Faith. God is not a respective person. What he did for me he can also do for you.

I begin writing this book before God sent my Boaz. He blessed me with an awesome man of God. One that is willing to love me beyond my faults, just as Jesus does. A few months after our marriage, this book was completed. However, I never got around to publishing it due to other circumstances until now. Our timing is not God's time. This is God's divine time for this manuscript. I hope you enjoy the work of the Lord.

Introduction

Today's women aren't like yesterday's women. The women of old were wise and they served God with all of their heart. They worked in the home and outside of the home. They respected their husbands and did him good. He could trust her because she was his helpmeet. They taught their children and nurtured them with the love of Christ. They dressed modestly and carried themselves in a way that was pleasing to God and respectful to their husbands. They mirrored the **Proverb 31** woman. Who can find a virtuous woman? For her price if far above rubies.

Many ladies of this world try hard to live up to what society portrays rather than the word of God. A half-dressed woman with slender build, long silky hair, and a large derriere equates to sexy. We as women degrade ourselves by dressing sleazy, fighting, and acting messy over things that aren't important. Many women today have provocative movements in dancing such as twerking and think that it can be used for their benefit. Many women speak un-lady like; steal to get the things they desire but cannot afford. They starve themselves and take all kinds of substances to get the Beyoncé and Ciara figures. Our bodies are our weapons; we use them to get the guys or the things that we want. Some women over eat due to the anxiety of not being able to have the person they want. So they fall into a state of depression and begin to abuse their bodies. Actions like these give other people the "OK" to degrade women as well. Many secular artists degrade women and many ladies dance and sing to their music. It is sad that we as a people have come to a point where we are accepting who others claim us to be instead of who God has called us to be. Women call one another out of their names and sometimes we will answer the call of nonsense.

World issues, societal views, and personal situations have caused us to forget and never search out what God says about us. We accept what others think and say about us. We don't have to live up to society nor do we have to make ourselves out to be something that we are not. I read a lot about different ones who have gone to Hollywood to pursue their career as an actor, model, producer, singer, or whatever. When they entered into that arena they were told that they had the talent but not the full package due to the outer appearance. The rejection left them hurt and struggling to become the person they are not. Even in the job market, a woman has a glass ceiling which only allows them to go so far up the chain. There are many women selling out for a position. No one shouldn't have to sleep around to get their needs met or to get a position. We are all fearfully and wonderfully made. We shouldn't have to flaunt ourselves just to be seen. We shouldn't have to change who we are. We should not have to lower our standards to get a position we deserve. As a human being we all "crave" attention. Attention touches our inner man so we desire it. Watch what you do to get attention. There is good attention and bad attention. The way you carry yourself determines the type of attention you will attract. Your dress, your talk, your appearance says a lot about your character. Be careful not to give the wrong impression.

Don't fret about being single, don't rush the process. As a single woman take advantage of this time. Go through the process with joy. You have to allow God to prove you. He can't send you his best from his treasure chest when you're not ready to receive that person. You will only mistreat them, misuse them, and eventually lose them. It is time to do a spiritual inspection and natural evaluations. Are you bearing fruit or are your fruits withering up and dying instantly? If you have intentions on one day becoming someone's' wife, how can you be a good wife when you don't even know yourself? Two shattered people don't make a whole. You just have a big shattered mess. Allow God to make you whole.

I know I am asking a lot of questions but look at it as a brain exercise. Some may say, I know myself, but do you really? Allow God to give you an assessment. Ask God for that self-evaluation exam. There are some things that you need and things that must be completed before moving to the next level. Just as you have pre-requisite classes that you must take and pass before moving to the next level, there are some things that must be mastered spiritually and naturally before moving into the position God has for you. On the other hand, there are some positions God will put you in and develop you while you are there.

It is time to wake up, take your place and allow God to develop you into who he has called you to be. All you have to do is step up to the plate. Accept your assignment and watch God move on your behalf.

Ruth, Naomi's daughter–in–law became a single lady due to life circumstances. She chose to live for a God that she didn't know. She trusted our one true and living God first and God sent her Boaz. I believe that if you true a God that you didn't know and seek Him first then will you see the manifestations of your prayers.

Do you trust God or have you moved ahead of him? Have you chosen someone or are you waiting on God?

> Being single is a ministry. It's a ministry of sanctification. My life is a testimony for the saved and single in the Lord. I even pray that it will minister to those that haven't accepted Christ as their Lord and Savior.
>
> They that wait upon the Lord shall renew their strength; they shall mount up with the wings as eagles; they shall run, and not be weary; they shall walk, and not faint (**Isaiah 40:31**).

Chapter 1

Chosen–My Testimony

Dear Single One:

Many are called but few are chosen. I am one of the chosen ones and so are you. We have been chosen to be translated from darkness into light. Being single is not a bad relationship status. It is not loneliness or boredom. It is actually a great position to be in. Being single is a ministry. It is not a mistake that you are in this position. God has you in this predicament for a reason and for a season. Maybe it is to draw you closer to him. It could be for Him to show you true love. Possibly God is trying to reveal to you your self–worth. It could be for a testimony or to allow you to experience an abundant life as a single person. Whatever the reason, it is working out for your good. Be content in your current lifestyle. Don't be anxious and so eager to move but stand still. God is moving on your behalf. He is preparing someone to receive you and arranging elements within your being to receive his very best. God knows exactly what you need in a mate, based on how he created you. It isn't his will to throw you into something just to say you're involved. Furthermore, why would you want to settle when you have someone handcrafted especially for you? As individuals we should want the best for ourselves. If we don't want the best for ourselves we can't expect for others to want the best for us.

I was born and raised in a small town in the south called Greenwood, MS. I like to say my siblings and I were raised in the church. We were sent to church every Sunday with our grandparents but like most children in the church, I would play during Sunday school and sleep during service. Unfortunately, I didn't learn much about the Lord so I couldn't live for him. I knew that Jesus died and he rose again on the third day and I knew that he loved me. I learned that from my Easter speeches. I learned that he had the whole world in his hand from a song. So Sunday mornings for me were just another day of playtime with my church buddies. My family and I never prayed together, never read our bibles, and we really never discussed God.

I grew up in a typical household of working parents and all the other family drama that many deal with. I don't recall my parents actually telling us that they loved us but their actions spoke it. I don't remember my father reaching out to me as a little girl telling me that I was beautiful, pretty, intelligent, or giving me positive affirmations. My father was more of a disciplinarian and he believed in tough love; beating first and talking second. I knew that if I disobeyed or disappointed my father I had to suffer the consequences. So I lived to please my father. I lived to please man. That characteristic of people pleasing followed me throughout my adult life until I was introduced to Jesus.

Many of the things I did in life were done to please others. Due to my lack of knowledge and faith in God, I lived in darkness and I was blind and empty for many years. I thought that people pleasing could fill the void invading the space within me. Whatever I had to do to satisfy that special someone in my life, I was willing to do it.

When it came to a relationship I craved being his most prized possession, the great accomplishment that had been engraved in my mate's heart. I wanted to be his forever. I tried to please my man on every level. If it took me getting out of character or defying my temple, I was willing. I wanted to cater to him by giving and doing all I could. Whenever I was in a relationship, I was selfless. I pushed my needs aside and I focused on the needs of my mate. I catered to his every need however, I wasn't treated the same. I was praying that I would be deemed special enough to be the number one to some man. Yet not facing the truth of how could he feel so highly of me when my actions displayed how lowly I felt about myself?

My self-esteem reflected in my willingness to settle for the sake of not being alone. Sometimes life gets hard. It can throw you some curve balls, there can be some stumbling blocks, and obstacles that will try to distract and divert your attention. Yet you want someone to share your life with.

The plans that we have set for our individual lives

may not go as we had in mind. Many times we will base those decisions and plans off of our experiences and perception of society. I have found that the lies of this world will have you losing focus on your whole purpose of existing. Everyone has a purpose in life. It is important that you realize your purpose and your reason for existing, for those to bring forth the beauty of you. Everyone has been given different gifts, talents, and different assignments. Yet, our primary focus is the same. Our purpose is to serve God; therefore, be content in whatever position God has you in. You can't want what other people have. You have to learn to walk your walk. Discontentment will have you forever wishing, hoping, and will always have you disappointed.

The older I got, the more I considered myself to be a strong independent black woman. I was well educated; I had a job, my own car, and my own place. I felt that I could take care of myself and didn't need anyone, when in reality I feared being alone. I craved for the consistent presence of a man. But in the cloudiness of my heart lived the hurt, pain, fear, frustration, misunderstanding, abuse, lack of love from all of those so-called relationships that I once gave my all. I was tired! Tired to the point that I deeply desired to just wash my hands with men altogether. That was merely a thought that held no realistic weight. I never had the courage or a real desire to be done with wanting a man. I felt I was the perfect pick for any man, so it was hard for me to understand the mistreatment that came through the lying, cheating, manipulation, and deceit. Fortunately, those were never characteristics I possessed, only the cards I had been dealt. My mom always told me

"Casey don't expect someone to treat you like you would treat them. You both were raised differently. You don't have to take mistreatment and you don't have to change your standards for anyone".

It seemed like love was all around me, yet real love never touched me. No matter where I was I would see couples hugging, kissing, and holding hands in public, having children, or getting married. I often questioned myself. "Why me? What makes it so hard for a man to fall in love with me? Why am I constantly giving my all to receive nothing in return?" It really hurt to feel as if I had been chosen as the unlovable one. I begin to question my weight, my intelligence, my skin color, my hair texture, and my overall appearance. It seemed like everybody had someone except me. My self-esteem was constantly diminishing.

I reflect back to 9th grade my friends and I would group up in a circle and talk about different things. The conversations always seemed to go towards love and sex. At that time I wasn't sexually active but the conversation was intriguing and appeasing to my flesh. Based on the perception of my peers, I thought sex naturally equaled to love. I was young and didn't know any better. In my search for love I found a boyfriend and the relationship lasted for a little more than 3years. I thought what we shared was actual love, so of course I gave him my most prized possession; my virginity at the age of 16. I was so blinded by this boy until I did what he wanted. He didn't have to manipulate me to do anything. I was just weak for him and weakness caused me to blindly believe that it was love at first sight. I loved him and he fulfilled me so I thought. I needed his validation and I found security in him; until the ultimate betrayal of cheating. His betrayal ran me into the arms of another man and I became pregnant at an early age of 19. I had plans for my life to succeed but a baby wasn't in those plans. The moment I found out I was expecting I was disappointed in myself but yet excited. I felt I didn't need the love of no one else. I had been giving an opportunity to give all of my love and attention to a child I created and he would give all of his love to me. I knew I would be able to experience an unfailing love through my child. I had solved this mystery thing called love; at least that's what I thought. Going against my parents' rules of shacking, I moved out of their house and I allowed my son's father to move in with me. And the cycle began again. Here I was eyes wide open but blinded by lust.

Once more I based my sense of worth on the affections and validation of a man. For God's sake, I had given my body to people I didn't love, to those I thought I loved, and those that didn't love me back. So I just couldn't wrap my head around not being good enough, especially with all that I had given up. Wasn't that supposed to make them stay? My heart was beginning to harden and my soul was becoming numb. These were my words. "I'm lonely, unhappy, and just frustrated with my situation. I'm nice, intelligent, and I think I am beautiful but men seem to mess over me". I began to say that so often, until I think I could have made a song. Every relationship I had ever been in had been a failure. I began to think it was me. I would play wifey and didn't have a ring, papers, or his last name. Seems like the more I tried to conform to the person these men desired me to be the unhappy I became. I begin to feel a way that I didn't want to feel. I was feeling lost. I desired change in myself. I needed to learn to put myself first and love me because those men that was once a part of my life wasn't changing. I found that if I wanted to see change, I had to be the change and stop settling and accepting anything.

Those men were never designed to be mine but I wanted to keep my man, a man who obviously didn't know who he was and who was battling insecurity himself. He couldn't give me what he was unfamiliar with. He was seeking to fill his cup, while he depleted mine. Man after man proved to be another failed attention. I wanted to be saved, but really those men needed to be saved themselves. I made sure my outer appearance looked the best yet the inner man was deteriorating. I made sure to dress right; sleazy if the occasion called for it. Hair whipped right, fake nails, and fine jewelry all for the wrong reasons. Nothing is wrong with taking care of you. I encourage you to do what makes you feel good but do it for yourself and not for others.

Because of my upbringing I knew that there was a God somewhere and I knew that I could talk to him. There were times I would pray for a mate. How crazy was that? Pray to a God that I didn't even know or wouldn't even serve. Yet, I had the audacity to part my lips and ask him for something that wasn't good for me. "Lord, I need a man. I need a man so I can feel complete. I need a man so my son would have a dad. Lord, I need a man so my sexual needs will be met. Lord I need a man for stability. Lord help me I need man. I would even say any man Lord but not a husband right now. I'm sure if you are reading this book, these thoughts have come across your mind before. Imagine praying prayers that didn't even make sense. I was so blinded by lust until I didn't know how to pray accurately. After examining myself, I found that the discomfort, unhappiness, depression and frustration I was feeling all stemmed from me not being myself because I didn't know myself.

What I needed was "THE ULTIMATE MAN" in my life. A man that would not lead me astray, one that would not spit game just to get next to my body, one that would not use me for his personal gain, and one that wouldn't just tell me he loves me without meaning it. I needed a man that was able and willing to prove it in his actions. I needed someone that could supply all of my needs and protect me from the things that weren't good for me. I also needed someone that would build me up and encourage me when I was down. I didn't need a temporary fix; I needed a fix that would be eternal. The more I searched the harder the search became. Finding that type of man seemed impossible. But I continued to search all over the clubs, grocery stores, churches, work, etc.

I played the role and also have been played in the process. I thought that having the right figure and the face to match, would win me "the" man. I found something out: just as I was trying hard to portray myself to be something that I was not, there are many more people doing the same. Gaining affections, recognitions, and acknowledgments is a game and there are so many people competing. I was tired of competing with others; I found that it was a losing battle. I wanted to be on a winning team so I began to work on myself.

One day I was asked to move to another state. In my quest to find the man that was mine I was willing to go because I felt I wasn't prospering in my current place. By this time, I had no job, no money, and I couldn't see my future there. The only thing I had going for myself was my son and my education, but even with a Bachelor's degree I couldn't find a job. I had lost my self-confidences, self-esteem, self-worth, and more. So I figured I had nothing to lose. I moved out of my comfort zone into a foreign land. The move was hard. It was only my sister, her family and I. Still I found myself in this foreign place with no job, no money, no man, and I had moved away from my family and friends. Many times I became the third wheel so to say whenever we went out. I suddenly slipped into depression. There were days I would only get out of bed to put my son on the bus and to get him off the bus. I was miserable and I hated the physical and emotional place I had landed in. My sister would tell me that if I was going to remain in her house I had to go to church on Sundays. That wasn't an issue because I was use to that anyway. However it was such a pull to press my way to the house of the Lord. I visited this small church a few days after being in town. The people there looked strange and they were doing strange things. Things like praising God, shouting, and running for Jesus. I thought they were insane. I had never been to a church where the people were so rowdy for God. My words were "It doesn't take all that". Little did I know at that time it wasn't them that was strange, it was me. The more I sat around the strangers the more I began to assimilate into strangeness of praising God. Association does bring about assimilation. I soon learned that wasn't anything strange about praising God. The bible tells us let everything that has breath Praise ye the Lord. This is exactly what they were doing. They were on fire for Jesus. I've always had a secret desire to have what they had but thinking of the things I had to give up and what people would think of me caused me not to accept Christ. After a few visits to this church, Jesus got a hold of me and I became like them. My soul began to catch on fire, the Holy Ghost got in me and I begin to speak in an unknown tongue, my feet got to stomping, and every opportunity I got I was running around the church. My insides were burning from the Holy Ghost and every time someone said "JESUS" tears would flow. I had experienced the new birth. I had truly had an encounter with Christ like never before. My spirit had been lifted.

I remember I gave my heart to Jesus back in 2001. However, the experience I had in 2001 can't compare to the experience I had in 2006. I wasn't ready in 2001, a backslider I became in only a few months

In 2006, at that moment of spiritual highness, I allowed God to move in. Instantly after the Holy Spirit took up residence he began to minister to my every need. I could actually hear the voice of God. I could see clearly. I could identify sin immediately and I knew that I wanted no part of that. I realized that it wasn't an earthly man I needed to fill that void but it was Christ. What I lacked most in my life was Christ. If you are feeling empty, low, and don't know which way to turn; Jesus is the answer. There is a void that only he can fill.

I accepted Christ as my personal savior. I built a relationship with him and he became my friend. The Lord began to build me up. He placed me around Godly women and I begin to see how they would dress modestly, carry themselves with dignity, and how they would address issues nicely and not with a nasty disposition. I stopped looking to celebrities to be my role model and idols. Jesus the most prestigious celebrity that has ever walked this earth became my role model. He has done what no other man has done. He turned water into wine and he feed 5,000 men with 5 loaves of bread and 2 fish. He healed the sick, opened blind eyes, made the lame to walk, and raised the dead. He is the only man to walk on water. Jesus saved my soul and alongside a host of other miracles. Jesus resume is impressive. That's the type of man that every person should want to know. Because of Jesus, I no longer have to compete in the world. I have triumphed over all of my competitors. I don't have to try to be the "trophy" woman of some earthly man because I am "the trophy" of God. Each of us are souvenirs of Christ's victory. We have been redeemed by the blood of the Lamb. He who accepts Christ, name has been written in the Lamb Book of Life. I am his eternal "trophy". My name is nicely printed.

God began to deal with me about self-confidence, self-worth, and maintaining my character. He began to speak and I began to write. I also found myself praying and mediating on his word day and night. So when the enemy would begin to operate in his tactics I had the word as well as worldly knowledge to see the things that I had looked over for so many years. I was able see on both ends. Overcoming the enemy's tactics of being single is a challenge but it is possible if you would believe and receive. God took me through a process of loving him and loving myself. Let him do the same for you. You are beautiful in God's eye. You are his creation and he makes no mistakes.

God told me and I tell you···STAND FIRM!

You don't need a man or a woman to complete you when you realize who you are, whose you are, your destiny and purpose for living. This is all that is needed to sustain in the less than normal world.

To All Singles A Message From God:

Singles where some of you are and where you should be.

Chapter 2

Accepting Christ– Salvation

The first class you must master in this thing called life is Salvation. This is the first and most important step to identification and being able to live the way called has God you to live.

The Greek word for salvation is "soteria", which means deliverance. Salvation means to be delivered from the bondage of sin, sickness, and diseases. You have been delivered from Satan's bondage so you no longer have to live in defeat. Salvation is simple and it has been given to the human race. The bible tells us in Jude 3 that salvation is common. In other words it's something that is done often. Many people have and will accept Christ as their Lord and savior. You have to cast down every evil thought that tells you "oh you have time" or "that's not for young people". Salvation is for everyone. As I am writing this book I believe there is someone in this world giving their heart to Jesus. God does not save based on criteria. All you have to do is believe in Christ and the death burial and resurrection and receive him in your heart. It is as simple as believing and altering your mind and heart. Jesus took the hard part: death on the cross and left the easy part: Salvation. What Jesus has done for us no other man could have done. I personally couldn't have taken the beating and the bruises for a world that received me not. I think that would be hard. Abraham was asked by God to sacrifice his only son as a burnt offering to him. It seemed as though he had a willing heart. The bible says that he rose up and went into the direction in which the Lord spoke unto him. He bound his son and built an altar to prepare his son as an offering. Just as he was about to slay him an angel spoke unto Abraham. God provided a ram in the bush. Can you image given your only child's life? God gave his only son with no reservation. He was slang for the sins of the world. Admit to yourself that you are a sinner. He died for you and I. No one is perfect, no matter how hard you try perfection is not in our reach. However we should always strive to do better. The bible tells us "for all have sinned and fallen short of the glory (**Romans 8:23**). All have sin; no one is exempt from sin, we were born with a sinful nature that automatically prompted us to sin. Have you ever wondered why wrong thoughts and actions follow you? It is the sinful nature within us. When God first made man he wasn't made to sin he was made in the image of Christ.

> "So God created man in his own image, in the image of God created he him; male and female created he them" (**Genesis 1:27**).

The word image in this scripture means the likeness or the resemblance. Think about it. Your child resemblance you in some way and you resemble your parents in some kind of way. We may act like our parents and the older we get we may even sound like them. Our children may have a lot of our characteristics as well. They may think like us, walk like us, and talk like us. If a DNA test was conducted on you and your child you will see that you have the same genetic make-up. If you have accepted Christ, God's DNA is flowing through you because he now resides in you. So you have no choice but to resemble him. You have the same spiritual genetic makeup. You should think like God, talk like God, and walk like God. Remember we are like God, but we are not God. So don't put him in a box and make God in your image. Don't try to make him the God you want. He will be the God that you need.

When Adam disobeyed God in the garden, his disobedience caused spiritual death over all. If you notice Genesis 3, when Eve ate from the tree nothing happen. When Adam ate from it both of their eyes were opened and they knew they were naked. This is where sin began.

> "Wherefore, as by one man sin entered Into the world, and death by sin; and so death passed upon all men, for that all have sinned" (Romans 5:12).

We inherited a sinful nature through our father Adam. We were all destined for death (HELL). Because of the act of one man, sin distorts our image, our likeness, our resemblance of God. We no longer looked like God. However, if I may say God had sympathy for us. He prepared his son a body, one that would be slain for you and me, so he could come and redeem man from the tyranny of Satan. "For God so love the world that he gave his only begotten son, that whosoever shall believe on him shall not perish but have everlasting life" (John 3:16).

He had all humanity in mind when he made this decision. God wants to restore your image. He no longer wants you to have a distorted view when you look into the mirror. He wants your image to be pure, holy, and without any blemishes. His blood cleans us up. All past, present, and future people would be saved from oppression of death. He so loved the world; he loved us unconditionally and pass our faults. It doesn't matter what color you are, your ethnicity, your gender, how rich or poor you are, how pretty or how fine you think you are. It doesn't matter what you have done in your past or how you have treated people. None of that matters to God. He loved man– kind so much. Unlike mankind, we base our love on looks, what someone can do for us, and our feelings. God's loves is absolute, so we don't have to worry about his love changing. God wanted our fellowship so he gave his son to be slain; so that he could gain many sons. He didn't take individual statuses and looks and determine who he was going to save. He chose each one of us, name by name. To be called a son of God only requires belief in the cross. Being confident in the success of the death, burial, and resurrection qualifies us to be God sons (daughters).

Accept Christ in your heart, believe that he died for your sins, and confess that Jesus Christ is Lord. Then you shall be saved.

> "That if thou shalt confess with thy mouth the Lord Jesus, and shalt believe in thine heart that God hath raised him from the dead, thou shalt be saved. For with the heart man believeth unto righteousness; and with the mouth confession is made unto salvation" (Romans 10:9–10).

You do not have to work for it or earn it by doing good

deeds. It is a free gift. Our ticket has already been purchased. Our time for criminal offensives has already been served. We simply have to believe and receive it.

As a child I loved to color and half draw. I wasn't a good artist but I knew that I made the prefect clouds, the prefect hands, and the prefect sun. So in every picture I made sure I drew those three things. I didn't know the significance of those pictures until later. The clouds represented clarity; the perfect hands represented the hand of God that was on my life. Because of my frequent church attending with my grandparents, I knew that God had the whole world in his hand that he loved me unconditional. So whatever situation I got myself into I knew to call on the SON for help and this was the reason for the sun being drawn and shining. God needed to get my attention and the way he did it was through a picture. He brought this back to my attention and gave me revelation of it once I accepted him. He was there all along. Sometimes we don't understand the significance of a thing but in due time God will reveal all.

I often would ask what made me so special that God saved me. I have never been on drugs, never an alcoholic, and never committed a real crime that would cause me to do real time. I'm not boosting but I am very appreciative of how God spared my life. I realized that because he spared me from those things I still had something that I needed to be saved and delivered from. I was bound in sin just like everyone else. Many have the testimony of being delivered from drugs, alcohol, and sickness but my testimony is that he delivered me from people, fornication, loneliness, from being gullible, depression, and I could go on and on. My testimony may not be the same as your testimony but whatever your testimony is, know that you was spared because of the love God has for you.

Salvation is a must. No matter how good off you think you may be, no matter how you have it; God is needed. The wonderful thing about salvation is that God saves us no matter how much money you have or what you can do. You don't have to worry about going into debt to purchase it. The debt has already been paid; it is Free. He does not force salvation on anyone nor does he manipulate you to say yes. It's his love that draws us. God never puts stipulations on who he will save. He is so loving and so mindful of man. Only God can take the bad from you and he replace it with so much good.

Pray this prayer:

"Father, I am a sinner and I have fallen short of the glory. I know I have done some things that were totally against you. You know all and you have seen all. God I ask that you will forgive me of my sin and my iniquities. Lord cleanse me of all unrighteousness. God I believe that you died on the cross for my sins and I believe that you were raised from the dead so I may live. I believe that you are coming back again. Lord I ask that you will come into my heart and be my God. Help me to turn from my wicked ways and seek your face daily. Live in me and through me. In Jesus Name, Amen."

Now that you have accepted salvation through Christ, a change will take place when Christ is the center of your attention. Once you have accepted Christ know that you have been set free. Remember that salvation means to be delivered. When you say YES to Jesus there is a change in living that has to take place. From this moment on never walk in defeat again. You may be wondering what is defeat and how do I walk in defeat. Defeat means to be overpowered, beaten, conquered, or crushed by your opponent (enemy). You walk in defeat by yielding to the sinful nature. Since we are in Christ it is impossible to be defeated because Jesus has won the battle and he holds the victory. Therefore we are Victorious over the enemy, conquerors in every circumstance, and over-comers in every situation. Satan has lost his place of authority. Knowing this, we are victorious over every thought and feeling that tries to come upon us. So you have to speak to every feeling.

The major problem with Christianity today is that we have not accepted our salvation as a gift. Salvation is the ultimate blessing. Not the car, the house, the money, or the companion; those are added benefits. We get excited for temporary blessings that will lose their value and fade away. True blessings are the spiritual things that can't be valued like salvation, eternal life, deliverance, healing, anointing, and etc. Often times, we talk about we got to get a blessing but God has already blessed us with every blessing in the heavenly realm. It is time to call those blessings into manifestation. How do you call those blessings into manifestation? You have to first believe and receive it. When Jesus was in his own town teaching they were all amazed, but with the same attitude they doubted his abilities because he was just a carpenter and Mary's boy to them. The people minds were stuck on what they knew about him and his past. Their thoughts hindered their ability to believe. Some people will be stuck on what they know about you and they won't be able move forward. They will also try to keep you in your past. Don't allow people words, thoughts, and beliefs of you hinder you. Jesus was amongst his own people and couldn't work miracles because of their unbelief. So in order to receive from God you have to first believe. Secondly, you need to be obedient. Isaiah stated that "If ye be willing and obedient, ye shall eat the good of the land (Isaiah 1:19). In other words you will be blessed because of your willingness and obedience. There are some promises from God that we just need to believe and receive. Whatsoever you shall ask in prayer, believing, you will receive (Matt. 21:22). The promises are done. Walk in obedience and understand what has already been given. Start thanking him. Praise God in Advance. You have to see it before you see it or you will never see it. Meaning you have to see those things in the spirit, possess them in your spirit or you will never see the manifestation of them. Jesus is our all and has already provided our all. It is imperative that you accept this fact and believe that you have been purchased by the blood of Jesus. There is no fee involved, no interest accruing, and not a principal balance for Salvation. It has been given to you and no one can take it from you. However you can let it go by selling out to the devil. It can be misappropriated with the lack of understanding. When we as the body of Christ get the concept of "free salvation" then we will stop looking and start receiving. If JCPenny's or Macy's were having a sale and posted an ad saying, "All king size comforters are free" we would go to the store without money and we will receive our comforters with no reservation and no plan of return". If BMW was giving away a free car and all you had to do was accept it what would you do? I would take the keys and drive off so fast. You have to have the same thought about salvation. Jesus said it is done, the price has been paid; receive your blessing of Salvation. Your ticket to Heaven has been paid. Don't miss out on your free gift. Grab hold of the things of God, accept them in your heart, and apply them to your life. Without understanding you set yourselves up to be used.

Salvation offers so much. Receive that thought and know that you are worth more than jewels. Now that you have accepted Christ a new level of demons will approach you. To be honest no person on earth can afford you and no demon in Hell can stop the movement of God for you. Stand strong!!! Pray without ceasing, meditate on the word day and night, fellowship with people of like faith, and consider fasting to bring your flesh subject to the spirit. Welcome to the Kingdom of God.

Chapter 3

Being Filled—Holy Spirit

The second pre-requisite for living a single life is receiving the Spirit of God which is the Holy Spirit. The Greek word for Holy Spirit is Pneuma which means wind, breathe, or spirit. Jesus died for our sins but it is the Holy Spirit that helps us to live for God. Before Jesus was crucified He promised his disciples that they would be given a gift of the Comforter, which is the Holy Spirit.

> "If ye love me, keep my commandments. And I will pray the Father, and he shall give you another Comforter, that he may abide with you forever; Even the Spirit of truth; whom the world cannot receive, because it seeth him not, neither knoweth him: but ye know him; for he dwelleth with you, and shall be in you (John 14:15-17)"

The Greek word for comforter is parakletos which means one who comes alongside to help. So the comforter is our help. The Holy Spirit is essential to your salvation. It is He that gives us the power to live a Christian life. The

Holy Spirit is the power that works within us. (Eph. 3:20)."
But ye shall receive power, after that the Holy Ghost is
come upon you" (Acts 1:8). In order for your home to have
working lights you have to have some energy from a power
source. In order for our light to shine we have to be
connected to the power source. Holy Spirit is a person. He
is the 3rd person of the Godhead. You have God the Father,
God the Son, and God the Holy Spirit. "For there are three
that bear record in heaven, the Father, the Word, and the
Holy Ghost: and these three are one (1John 5:7)". The
word trinity is not in the bible. However, we believe that
there are three entities but one God. The Holy Spirit is the
Spirit of God. God the Father and God the Son was at the
beginning of creations so was the Holy Spirit. **Genesis 1:2,**
"The spirit of God moved upon the face of the waters". We
find a lot about the Holy Spirit and his role from the word
of God. We know that Holy Spirit dwells in us and he is
our Power.

Prior to anyone accepting Christ the pre-work of
Salvation is done. The Holy Spirit sets the foundation for
people to accept the Gospel. He speaks through individuals
when preaching the Gospel truths. The word of God
penetrates the hearts and souls of people. A few years
before I gave my life to Christ, I could actual see the pre-
work of Salvation that was occurring in my life by the Holy
Spirit. I begin to feel convicted when I was doing wrong
things. I really couldn't understand why I was so emotional
about things that I once did with no conviction. There were
times I would stop in the middle of my sin and cry and ask
God for forgiveness. At that time I did not know anything
about the Holy Spirit. I knew that God was real but it

never settled in my mind that it was the Lord that was working on me.

When I joined the church I spoke about earlier, my Pastor's wife lead me to Christ. She asked if I wanted to be filled with the Holy Spirit and that the evidence of the Holy Spirit would be the ability to speak in unknown tongues. At that time I said no because I was once told speaking in tongue was not of God. Out of my lack of knowledge I rejected God. But thank God for second chances. A few weeks past, a traveling Evangelist visited our church and delivered a powerful message about God's protection and love. The word of God hit me and before I knew it I was in tears. At that moment, my first lady asked again if I wanted to be filled with the Holy Spirit. I don't remember answering her and I don't remember going to the altar. I remember the moment she laid her hands on me and I began to cry uncontrollably. Suddenly I began to speak in a stammering tongue that I didn't understand. My mind wanted to cut it off but I couldn't. It was beyond my control. It was an experience I had never imagined or felt before.

And these signs shall follow them that believe···They shall speak with new tongues···(Mark 16:17).

Once I received the Holy Spirit, I recalled crying every time someone said the name of Jesus. My hunger and thirst after righteousness increased. I started to read God's word daily. I began to set aside a time to give God my undivided attention in prayer. I began to learn God through the power of the Holy Spirit. It is important that you learn God for yourselves. You can't take what someone tells you and run with it. Search it out for yourself. The Holy Spirit was and is a vital part of our salvation and learning God includes learning about His spirit.

You have to know the Spirit of God. The Spirit of God is what dwells in us. We have to learn to listen to his spirit because it is his job to lead and guide us in all truth. Learning the Spirit of God is a process. It is percepts upon percepts, line upon line; here a little there a little (Is. 28:11). You will not get everything all at once but it is gradual. There is no set formula on how to master the learning of God but the more you avail yourself to the Spirit of God, the more you will learn of Him. Your confidence in the Spirit of God will grow and manifest.

On this journey of single living learn who the Holy Spirit is to you. He will help you on this walk. Learn how to acknowledge him in your life. He will help you keep yourself pure even when it seem like all odds are against you. He is your power to say No to sin and Yes to God. The Holy Spirit has many roles and characteristics and he is a gift to each one of us in many ways: some not all are listed below.

1. He was left to us as a comforter and our teacher.

> But the Comforter, which is the Holy Ghost, whom the Father will send in my name, he shall teach you all things, and bring all things to your remembrance, whatsoever I have said unto you. (John 14:26)

2. Holy Spirit is the truth and he is our guide. He will reveal all things to us.

> Howbeit when he, the Spirit of truth, is come,
> he will guide you into all truth: for he shall
> not speak of himself; but whatsoever he shall
> hear, that shall he speak: and he will show
> you things to come. (John 16:13)

3. Holy Spirit is intelligent.

> But God hath revealed them unto us by his
> Spirit: for the Spirit searcheth all things, yea,
> the deep things of God. For what man
> knoweth the things of a man, save the spirit of
> man which is in him? even so the things of
> God knoweth no man, but the Spirit of God.
> (1 Cor. 2:10–11)

4. Holy Spirit has emotions and we should not grieve
   him.

> And grieve not the Holy Spirit of God,
> whereby ye are sealed unto the day of
> redemption. (Eph 4:30).

5. Holy Spirit intercedes for us in prayer.

> Likewise the Spirit also helpeth our
> infirmities: for we know not what we should
> pray for as we ought: but the Spirit itself
> maketh intercession for us with groanings
> which cannot be uttered (Romans 8:26)

If you want to receive the Holy Spirit, all you have to do is
ask for Him.

> "For every one that asketh receiveth; and he that

seeketh findeth; and to him that knocketh it shall be opened. If a son shall ask bread of any of you that is a father, will he give him a stone? or if he ask a fish, will he for a fish give him a serpent? Or if he shall ask an egg, will he offer him a scorpion? If ye then, being evil, know how to give good gifts unto your children: how much more shall your heavenly Father give the Holy Spirit to them that ask him? (Luke 10:11–13)"

We can't be afraid of the Holy Spirit. He will not tempt us with evil nor would he do anything to destroy us or hurt us. He is a leader. He guides us and strengthens us in this Christian walk. God is ready and willing to give to you. He will not withhold no good thing from you, but it begins with you believing and asking. We have been bought with a price. Trust in our Savior. "In whom ye also trusted, after that ye heard the word of truth, the gospel of your salvation: in whom also after that ye believed, ye were sealed with that Holy Spirit of promise, Which is the earnest of our inheritance until the redemption of the purchased possession, unto the praise of his glory. (Eph 1:13–14). The Holy Spirit is our down payment of our inheritance. Ask for God's spirit to live in you.

Pray this prayer:

Father I have accepted you as my Lord and Savior but God I need to be sealed with your precious Holy Spirit. I know that the Holy Spirit is my power source. God I need your power to sustain me throughout this life. Feel me with your Holy Spirit and by faith I receive. I want to speak in those unknown tongue as evidence. God empower me for service. God I believe that I have received all of you. In Jesus Name I pray.

Amen

Chapter 4

Transformation– Renew the Mind

"I beseech you therefore, brethren, by the mercies of God, that ye present your bodies a living sacrifice, holy, acceptable unto God, which is your reasonable service. And be not conformed to this world: but be ye transformed by the renewing of your mind, that ye may prove what is that good, and acceptable, and perfect, will of God.(Romans 12:1-2)."

God has some requirements for your life but in order to be able to live up to what he is calling you to do; you have to stop conforming and allow your mind to be transformed. When I think of the word transformation an image of the transformers enter into my mind. In the movie Transformers, the motor vehicles had the ability to totally change their appearance. The outcome of their changed appearance prepared them for war. This is the way it should be when we have accepted Christ. There should be a visible change in our lives that will prepare us for spiritual war. To transform, is to make a dramatic alteration. The third pre requisite for living single is having your mind renewed. When you come to Christ it is best to lose your mind and gain the mind of Christ.

"For they that are after the flesh do mind the things of the flesh; but they that are after the Spirit the things of the Spirit. For to be carnally minded is death; but to be spiritually minded is life and peace (Romans 8:6-7)."

In this walk with Christ, we cannot continue to rely on our own thoughts. To have a mind of the flesh would bring about spiritual death and eventually physical death. When you are carnally minded it is so easy to be led astray. You think and view things from a worldly viewpoint instead of a spiritual prospective. A carnal mind will have you double minded and unaware of what the Lord is saying.

Your mind is like the devil's playground. His plots and plans involve nothing but sin. He uses your mind to accomplish his tasks of death and deception. Satan is the father of lies. He would start off with little things that seem innocent like a love song by your favorite artist or a love story on television. Suddenly, you find yourself reminiscing on the past with Billy, Bob, Jane, Sally, and whoever. Then before you know it you are on the phone inviting Joe Blow out or Sally Sue over for a dinner and movie. All the while, Satan is setting you up for destruction. Be careful what you let enter in your spirit. You have to do away with the old things. You were set free when you accepted Christ in your life. The enemy will plant a seed and have you saying, "I'm strong. I can invite him or her over and I will be ok." Remember he is like a roaring lion. He will wait until you are at your vulnerable point. At the point when you are lonely, bored, feeling unloved. Do not be entangled in your mind. Remember sin brings about spiritual death and separation from God. Be spiritual minded. Allow your mind to submit to the Godly influence. Follow God's lead. His path will give you light and life more abundantly. You will have a life that is worth living. Since you have a new life you have to let the things in the past go. Things of the past can fill your mind and spirit with lustful desires and bitterness. Don't allow your past to enter into your future. Let go of old baggage. It is worn out and it will wear you out.

> You are new creations, old things has passed and all things have become new and of God (2 Cor. 5:17).

Those things that you did before you perfect the first step of being single, I'm sure they weren't of God. Since they weren't of God they are all dead. Worldly songs, worldly friends, that worldly dress, the worldly talk and walk is not of God. You can't put new wine in old wine skin. The book of Ephesians says:

> " That ye put off concerning the former conversation the old man, which is corrupt according to the deceitful lusts; And be renewed in the spirit of your mind; And that ye put on the new man, which after God is created in righteousness and true holiness (Ephesians 4: 22-24).

Renewing your mind leads you to take action. You will want to change. You should be at a point in your life now where conversations are uneasy, some friendships are uncomfortable, and some places no longer interest you. There should be a change in progress. Those worldly conversations that you and your girls or boys use to engage in; cease now says the Lord. It doesn't matter what it was it can no longer be. Those conversations are your former manner of life: what you spoke, how you acted, and the way you dressed. God said to put it off; let it go, lay it down, do away with it, all of those things that concern the old man. The old man is the man that had the depraved sin nature. He was deceitful and led by the devil. He was filled with the lust of the eye, the lust of the flesh, and the pride of life. That man is dead. God said to put it off and be renewed in the Spirit of your mind. Having a renewed mind gives you strength. With the Holy Spirit, you will keep your mind focused on what is right. With a renewed mind, you will continue on the path of righteousness and it shall become easy to bury the old man and keep him buried.

My funeral obituary of an old man would go something like this:

DEATH & BURIAL OF OLD THINGS & RESURRECTION OF NEW THINGS

We have gathered here today to lay to rest Old Things. Old Things were born when I first entered into this world (sinful nature). Old Things lived where I lived and died where I live today. Old Things lived a long life. Life was full of ups and downs, heart aches and pains, disappointments and disillusions, and even brought some trouble and destroyed some relationships. Old things followed me around making me feel ashamed, less than, and worthless. Old Things brought along habits, addictions, bad friendships, and devices that was hard to shake.

Old Things matriculated through the school of the hard-knocks and gained useless experiences from The World Corporation. Satan was the President of the Company and Demons were the Principal of the Schools it attended. Old Things had a great impact. Old Things got many earthly awards but will never receive the Heavenly rewards.

Old Things took to death with it—lying, cheating, stealing, lack, poverty, old relationship, bad habits, worldly ways, drinking, smoking, profanity, provocative dressing, fornication, adultery, idolatry, low self—esteem, depression , oppression, manipulation, deception, pride, greed, lust of the eye, lust of the flesh, pride of life, uncleanliness, witchcraft, hatred, strife, heresies, seditions, wrath, sexual immortality, lasciviousness, jealousy, envy, and such likes.

Old Things are in a better place; DEAD and BURIED. Old Things leave only a vain memory that has no place in life. Old Things deeds have been mortified by the Blood of Jesus.

Old Things has passed away so the survival of New Things can take its place.

Adios Old Things, I'm repenting today and allowing New Things to step into place. Jesus has a greater impact for me and in me. Welcome Jesus. Hello salvation & deliverance. Good Morning, restoration and reconciliation. I receive you grace & mercy, holiness & humility. I accept and give love, joy, peace, long suffering, gentleness, goodness, faith, meekness, and temperance. I embrace healing, power, and victory. I appreciate and appropriate the blood that was shed on Calvary. Jesus does heal all wounds.

"I AM A NEW CREATION"

I wrote this as an encouragement to myself. I taped it on my mirror and this was something I spoke into my life daily. I urge you to do the same. Let the old you die. Leave it in a place to rest so that God can develop and raise the new you. You have to speak over yourself positive affirmations daily. Remind yourself who God is making and molding you to be. The mind has to be renewed to establish a Christ like mind. Having the mind of Christ helps us to have the spirit of Christ. The mind of Christ produces the spirit of Christ.

> "But the fruit of the Spirit is love, joy, peace, long-suffering, gentleness, goodness, faith, Meekness, temperance: against such there is no law (Gal 5:22-23)."

Establish Godly thoughts. In order to establish his thoughts you have to have revelation of him. Revelation of God comes from having an inmate relationship with him. You have to meditate (roll over in your mind) on his word day and night. Renewing the mind is a process and it requires personal discipline. Think about it. Over the years we have been programmed to think naturally and/or worldly. These worldly thoughts come from educational system, political view, society, family, friends, religions, books, and so on. Because of the depravity of our knowledge, there will be some struggles to transform into spiritual thinking.

I think about how we go through at 13 years of learning from Kindergarten to 12th grade. If you decide to further your education you can go for another 4-8years or more. In those years, we learn book knowledge, life skills, etc. We learn a lot of things, many things that we may never use again in life. There are very few that learned the word of God from school. The schools impact you with all of these things. It took years to learn most of the things we have stored in our minds. It may not be an overnight process to release them. Just as you had to study and drill knowledge in your mind for a test, you have to do the same now. Study and drill the word of God in your mind so your mindset can be renewed. We don't have to learn and study on our own; we have help. God has left us a comforter, the Holy Spirit to help. It will not happen overnight but begin now to discipline your mind. Train and discipline yourself for the purpose of Godliness. Give yourself only to God. Pursue a life of praying, fasting, studying the word, and going to church. I believe that you can do it and you will make it.

Seek God in prayer. Learn to pray effectively by incorporating the word of God. Prayer builds your relationship with God. You can learn God and his personality through prayer. Pray for a renewed mind. Pray that your mind would line up to the will of God for your life.

Pray this prayer:

"Father in the name of Jesus, I ask you Lord to renew my mind. God give me the desire to seek your face so I may hunger and thirst after righteousness. Lord I know that I am a new creation and old things have passed away. Help me to appropriate that fact. Lord I was made in your image; however, over the years I have lost sight of that. Restore my righteous mind and create in me a clean heart. God clear my mind of every evil thought and deed. Give me peace in my mind. Give me the mind of Christ so I can think like you Lord. In Jesus name I pray."

In this prayer you are identifying your faults, expression your spiritual desires and acknowledging that you can't do it without him.

Chapter 5

Walking In-Holiness

At times this Christian walk can be a little challenging and intense but it's enjoyable. God has some demands and requirements for us. Some are easy and some are hard to follow. Holiness is a demand whether you are single or married. Many times in life we hear people say, "Be Holy because we serve a Holy God," but they never tell you how to be Holy. I have even heard the church say it is still Holiness or Hell but they don't ever explain what Holiness is. Holiness is a separation from sin and a separation to God. God clearly defines Holiness, which is your manner of life throughout his word. Holiness is loving what God loves and hating what he hates; measuring everything in the world according to God's perspective, and never compromising.

"But as he which hath called you is holy, so be ye holy in all manner of conversation; because it is written, Be ye holy; for I am holy (**1 Peter 1:15-16**)."

This scripture is addressed to all Christians. Often times we as Christians think that it is impossible to be Holy. If it was impossible, God would have never said be Holy. God never requires anything from you that He didn't first give to you. Holiness is the purpose of Jesus being manifested in man. He came to take away sin so we might be Holy, made righteousness, and be in right standing with our Father God. In the Old Testament we see how nations were corrupt. They worshipped other gods, were killing babies, and marrying people they weren't supposed to marry. These same things are going on today. Holiness was a requirement then and it is still a requirement today. We have the Holy Spirit that was left as a Comforter living on the inside that helps us to show an outward expression of Holiness. The Holy Spirit helps us to reflect the image by which we were created: God's image.

> "So God created man in his own image, in the image of God created he him; male and female created he them (**Gen 1:27**)."

Therefore if we claim to be one of God's children then we should be like him. Holiness is a characteristic of God, and holiness is our pathway to abiding in His light.

> "God is light, in Him there is no darkness. No evil and no sin dwells in God, and God lives in us so let no sin or evil dwell in you"(**1 John 1:5**).

God defines holiness in both the Old and New testaments. In the book of Exodus Moses went up on the Mountain to commune with God, the Lord spoke a word to Moses about the House of Jacob and the children of Israel. He said, "Now therefore, if ye will obey my voice indeed, and keep my covenant, then ye shall be a peculiar treasure unto me above all people: for all the earth is mine: And ye shall be unto me a kingdom of priests, and a holy nation. These are the words which thou shalt speak unto the children of Israel" (19:5–6). Then in Exodus 20 God went on to give the commandments. The obedience of his commandments is what qualified Israel to be a Holy nation.

God also told us in the New Testament that we are "a chosen generation, a royal priesthood, a holy nation, a peculiar people; that ye should shew forth the praises of him who hath called you out of darkness into his marvelous light" (1 Peter 2:9). Paul was talking to the Hebrews because they were known to be a nation consecrated for God. We are Peculiar people. Why would God call us peculiar? Peculiar mean to be distinct from others. We are distinct. We are the salt of the earth, and a light that sits on top of a city. I talked in a previous chapter about how the people at the church I went to were praising God and it seemed strange to me. They are considered peculiar people and they are distinct from others. We are God's possessions; we have been bought and redeemed from sin by the blood of Jesus Christ. For this reason we are unique and we are set apart from this world's sin and have been separated unto righteousness. We no longer live in darkness which is sin because we have been called out from amongst the dark and translated "transferred" into light which is the full knowledge of God.

We have to be careful that we are not engaging in things that are holy like praying, fasting, studying, and going to church with an unclean heart. Just because we go to church on Sundays, pray sometimes, go periods without eating, and occasionally read God's word, does not make us Holy. We have to make sure that our actions and our heart are separated from the world and dedicated to God. To have one and not the other is simply unholy. That's just like saying that you are saved, but creeping with the devil. You're saved or you're not; either you're Holy or you're not. Holiness requires dedication and consecration to God. It is a Christian responsibility to walk in Holiness, for we will be judged for our decisions. You have control over the choices you make. Make a personal commitment to yourself daily that you will live a Holy life. Just as you gave yourself to sin, give yourself to holiness.

Your actions, your attitudes, and desires should be Holy. God is calling his church back to Holiness. You are the church, I am the church, and God's human creation is the church. Keep the church pure and holy. As a single person of God, sanctify yourself, be Holy. God is serious and it is vital for your life to attain the nature of God, or you will not see God. "Follow peace with all men, and holiness, without which no man shall see the Lord:" (Heb 12:14). Thoughts and anticipation of being married at times when God has not appointed those thoughts can kick you off your holy grounds. You will find yourself planning a future with an unknown individual and reminiscing on thoughts that's not from God then your heart will begin to get entangled. Lust will contain you. Lust has it way of tangling you up in a knot and it will be hard to break a loose. Then you will begin to walk in ungodliness. I was once entangled. I knew I loved God, I was living for him, but I secretly desired a guy that I knew wasn't for me. I had thoughts of him being my mate forever. Slowly I was drifting away from God. It took some long praying and fasting to get delivered from him. If you are not at that point, God is able to deliver you. God wants us to get real and focus on success in Holiness rather than success in natural things.

Pray this Prayer:

Father God, I have a desire to be holy. I have accepted you as my personal Savior and I have the Holy Spirit living on the inside. I know that you don't require anything from me that you didn't first give to me, but God I need help. Help me to be obedient to your Word and allow the Holy Spirit to lead me in all righteousness. I make a personal commitment to you today that I will live a holy life unto you Lord. I will not yield my temple to any ungodly acts. Lord I will keep your commandments and I will show forth praises to you. When I do things you have called me to do Lord I will do them with a clean heart and in the right spirit so they will be seen as holy to you. Holiness is what has been mandated to keep in relation with you. Therefore holiness is how I will live. God I thank you and praise you for including me as part of the peculiar people and the Holy nation. Lord help me when I fall short and help me to live totally for you, Father I give you honor, praise, and glory. In Jesus Name. Amen!

Chapter 6

Saving Yourself—Celibacy For Christ

Everyone is not called to be celibate. I do believe that there are some people God may have chosen to be celibate for life. In fact he has already graced them with the ability to do so. They will have the ability to control sexual desires. However, if you are not married celibacy is a requirement for salvation. On the flip side, fornication is a sin and will keep you from God. Therefore, being celibate becomes a personal choice.

> "Now the works of the flesh are manifest, which are these: Adultery, fornication, uncleanness, lasciviousness, Idolatry, witchcraft, hatred, variance, emulations, wrath, strife, seditions, heresies, Envying, murders, drunkenness, revelings, and such like: of the which I tell you before, as I have also told you in time past, that they which do such things shall not inherit the kingdom of God." (Gal 5:19–21).

Our desire is to make Heaven our home someday. However allowing our flesh to lead and guide us will not get us there. The flesh manifests things that are contrary to our Father. Feeling and urges will try to creep in and make you react. How do you stay on your guard and not follow those urges and feeling? By being prayerful and watchful.

> "Know ye not that the unrighteous shall not inherit the kingdom of God? Be not deceived: neither fornicators, nor idolaters, nor adulterers, nor effeminate, nor abusers of themselves with mankind, Nor thieves, nor covetous, nor drunkards, nor revilers, nor extortioners, shall inherit the kingdom of God" (1 Cor. 6:9-10).

God tells us that it is not good for man to be alone and He honors that through marriage. Sex was implemented for marriage to multiply and be fruitful. Yet, because so many people abuse it, sexual intercourse has been so perverted. So many times God would put people in our lives for a reason but we abuse the relationship by being intimate. Personally, I know I abused some relationships in my before Christ days for the very reason of intimacy or lustfulness. You may have regrets of not saving yourself, which is a very common regret among many. We have to come to a point in our lives where we stop laying down for every man that whispers sweet "nothings" in your ear. The talk of a sinner is simply NOTHING. It is designed to keep you trapped in sin. He's hurting and you are hurting and you both think that sexual intimacy will heal brokenness.

Sex is a big responsibility. When operated outside of marriage, it has so many consequences. Every person that you lay with leaves a part of their spirit within you. Now you have setup a war zone for your spirit man. The fight within is real. Your spirit is at war with your flesh. As for women, there are emotional attachments. It is hard for most women to just move on once we have given out. Our hearts get entangled, which also can entangle our minds. My parents always told me to be careful because you can get pregnant and catch sexual transmitted diseases but never once told me about the embodied spirits that would live within. The moment this happens and we recognize something is wrong then we want to pray and ask God to cure us or forgive us. But when we were caught up, God was the furthest person from our mind. Nothing is wrong with asking for forgiveness, but we have to be proactive thinkers. Sex outside of marriage is not worth the consequences. There are so many people young and old losing their lives from complications of HIV and other sexually transmitted diseases. The number of children being born out of wedlock has increased. There are babies having babies and fatherless children all around. There are young women that are incarcerated for life because they committed a crime of passion. There are so many men in prison because of domestic abuse and murdering a significant other. I recently read an article online, about a 15 year old girl who was cut in her face seven times by a 19 year old college student. The 19 year old college student found out her boyfriend was cheating on her for the 15 year old. This is a sad situation. The 15 year old is now left with scares in her face possibly forever. Even if she has plastic surgery she is still scarred for life. The 19 year old girl is in jail probably for a long time; her future has come to a halt all because of emotional ties that caused her to act before thinking. Both of their lives were disrupted at a young age because of emotional attachments.

Then there are those that are in bad relationship because of the emotions. Many are stuck in relationships and accepting physical, mental, and verbal abuse. This is where our women and men have gone wrong. We as people are allowing others to determine and dictate our lives. We have to stop letting others deem us as invaluable. This is a prime example of how we as women are emotionally attached. I agree with the saying that love will make you do some strange things. Look around at the evil in the world; most of the time it is due to a lack of love and misunderstanding of love. There is a difference in true love and what we mistake as love. Understanding true love is a mystery. We get it confused with what we have experienced in this world and the way we feel. God's love is true. The love of Christ can be strange sometimes to us. The only difference is, Christ's love is never evil and it never fails. God may have you doing something nice for your enemy and you don't even realize it or understand why.

Someone once told me about the strange love of Christ. I was the new girl on my job and it seemed as if I was the one to be picked on. I was talked down too, looked over, and mistreated. Many days I would leave work feeling very frustrated and sometimes with tears in my eyes. Being a new babe in Christ I felt that I should just be quite and not react the way the old person would act. I wanted to quit so badly but I needed the job. Day after day for months one particular lady would talk so bad to me about my work ethic. Being the new girl in the office with half training I made a few mistakes, but not enough to make a person behave the way this lady would. Not really understanding my Christian faith, my first reaction was not to pray; but cry. Eventually I learned to pray. I began to pray so hard one day because sitting in silence and taking the mistreatment from that lady began to get hard and I was on the verge of reacting outside of God. This was the first time I recognize the voice of God. God told me to treat the lady with the love of God; which I thought I was doing. God told me to treat her to lunch. Yes, strange love. God wanted me to show love to my enemy. It was a hard task to do but I did it. God will have you to show love in the midst of the enemy's tactics just so God can get the Glory. Out of obedience the lady and I have the best relationship that one could ever imagine now.

Often time singles are looked at as an outcast. I had plenty of people approach me asking why aren't you married? What are you waiting on? Why are you single? Just because you are single doesn't mean that something is wrong with you. Yet, the enemy will paint a picture of reasons why you are single. He will put in your mind you are single because of your looks, your beliefs, your family, and other nonsense. Know that you are single for a reason, but his reasons are not true. There are some great examples of people in the bible that were single. Some specifically stated they were single, some we assume because a spouse was never mentioned, and many widows that never remarried. From the Old and the New Testaments, singleness was just as common as marriage. For example, Joseph was the son of Jacob who was a dreamer and he had a gift of interpreting dreams. His gift landed him a leadership position in Egypt. He went from prison to the palace and he was single. Miriam, Moses's sister, there was never a spouse mentioned for her. The prophet Elijah was single and was the only person mentioned in the bible that was taken up to Heaven by a whirlwind. His successor, Elisha was also single. He left his mother and father and followed Elijah and God blessed him with a double portion of Elijah's spirit. Jeremiah was ordered by God not to marry. Jesus' friends Mary, Martha, and Lazarus, spouses were never mentioned for them but from the story of Lazarus we could tell that the three of them were a close knit family. Therefore, I would think that their spouses would have been mentioned. The Apostle Paul rejoiced because he was single. He said that he wish all was single like him but he understood that God gave everyone different gifts. He also tells us if you can't control your sexual urges then you should marry. Paul said that it is best not to marry (1Cor. 2-9). Jesus, our Savior, was the most prominent person in the Bible that was single. Jesus said that singleness is a gift from God. Jesus said if you marry, you should never divorce. Jesus and Paul thought alike. They both agreed that it is good not to marry but they understood that being single wasn't for everyone (Mt. 19:9-12). Then there were those widows in the Bible like Naomi that never remarried. There are others characters from the Bible that choose to live a single life for whatever reason. All of these people trusted and followed God. There were some standing on the promises of God and believing that he would bring them a spouse even in an older age. There were some people who had to leave their spouses behind to accomplish God's work such as Moses.

We can see from all of the various examples in the Bible that we too have to stand on the promise of God and wait on him to bring us someone or operate in the gift of celibacy. Being single is not something that just came about in our days but it was something that was happening before Christ walked this earth. Being single is a gift. Be content where God has you. Remember you are there for a reason.

If you are one that feels you have to have that pleasure,

then marry. It is better to marry than burn (1Cor.7:8-10). It is better to wait on God and allow him to give you someone then to run out and grab anybody. Don't be so eager to get married and miss the person that God has for you because you couldn't wait. You don't want to be involved with the wrong person for the rest of your life. If you do not want to marry, pray that God will give you the ability to be celibate. He is able to take away every desire, every feeling, and he is able to change your hormones. Surrender to the Lord. God is calling his people to holiness.

Pray this prayer:

Father, I pray that you will take every sexual lustful desire out of me. Just as you are renewing my mind, renew my body and make it brand new again. God make it so I will not lust after ungodly acts. Freeze the hormones that cause arousals and exotic desires. God don't restore my desires until the appropriate time. Lord I present my body to you as a living sacrifice, holy without blemishes, acceptable unto to you. Lord I ask for purification. Purge me and erase every pleasurable memory. When the enemy tries to bring it back Lord help me to talk back to the enemy and stand on your promises that I am a new creation. Old things have passed away and all things have become new and of God. I thank you for renewing my spirit, sanctifying my desire, and for being my husband. I love you Lord in Jesus name.

Chapter 7

Waiting On God

When should you wait, how should you wait, what should you do while you what, why should you wait···

Sometimes we will wait on everybody and everything except God. We put a time limit on prayer, but we will talk on the phone for hours to friends and family. We put a time limit on how long and how often we should worship in a service, yet most work 8hrs per day, 40 hrs per week. We put a time limit on when God should move in a situation, but we will wait on our love ones to move in their own timing. I can attest that waiting is hard and I once had no patience. I understand now that patience is a virtue. It is a valuable asset in life. We have to learn how to wait. Being impatient will cause you to step ahead of God and have you in undesirable situations. There are times on this journey that you will feel that you can't wait any longer. Your patience may be weighing thin. You may feel that your clock is ticking and it may seem like everyone around you is moving forward in a relationship and other things except you. But at that moment know that God said···.

"they that wait upon the Lord shall renew their strength, they shall run and not be weary; they shall mount up with wings like Eagles, they shall walk and not faint" (Isaiah 40:31). We have to learn how to wait. I know that with the speed of the world it is almost impossible to wait but if we possess the fruit of God's spirit then we can do it. One of the fruit of the spirit is long suffering. Learn to be long suffering in every situation. Remember God does not have a tool with numbers on it that measures time as we do. Time for him is eternal. One day is like a thousand years to the Lord, and a thousand years is like a day. So just because it's been 1 day to you doesn't matter to God. He dwells outside of time so he is always on time. He sees all and knows all. There is protection in delay. There is security in a "NO". God knows the future and he knows what is waiting ahead.

A young boy asks his mom one day, "Mom does God fast forward and rewind our lives like we do CD's and movies?" That was a very profound question. God is so powerful and He has the ability and the power to do as he pleases. He knew us before we were even formed in our mother's womb. Therefore He knows everything about us and about every situation. This is a question that we would never know the answer to but it is a good thought. God may be yet fast forwarding or rewinding your life now to avoid some of the headache and pain that lays waiting for you. Just go with the flow of God and have patience. We should forever wait on God in every situation. It is sad that often times we get ahead of God. Then we find ourselves in all kinds of mess and looking for God to clean it up. God is always on time according to his plan and his will. Slow down your time is near.

Sometimes in God we find ourselves getting impatient.

As I mentioned earlier, long suffering is important. It is important that we possess this fruit. As God is long suffering with us, then we should be long suffering also. Long suffering is an act of patiently waiting and enduring in hard and unhappy times. However having that quality is not what's important; instead, it is how one acts while they are waiting. A person that truly has this gift will wait and in the midst of waiting they will not lose their temper or give up. When you complain in the midst of the wait, it only makes the wait longer.

Let's consider the children of Israel. They were in the wilderness for 40 years. Imagine if they weren't murmuring and complaining and their lack of faith wasn't absent, they probably would have made it to the promise land much sooner. Consider Abraham and Sarah, not only did they doubt God, but they also didn't have patience to wait on the Lord. Sarah thought it was best if she helped God bring his promise to pass. So she sent her darling handmaiden in to sleep with her husband so they could conceive the child that had been promised to them. This was not the son God intended for them. Unfortunately, in the midst of helping God she created a mess that we are yet dealing with today. Descendants of Ishmael are in the modern day country called Iraq. Sometimes we get impatient and have children out of wedlock thinking and hoping that man will be there with us and for us. Unfortunately it is just a wishful thought.

Joseph had a dream that one day he would be a leader. He waited patiently on the Lord to move. Even in the midst of calamity in his life he never complained and never left the Lord. He remained faithful. He waited on the promises of God to be fulfilled. Whatever the Lord has told you or shown you, wait patiently on the Lord's promises to be fulfilled. Continue to do the work of the Lord even if you don't see the progression of the promise. Just trust and believe that God is no liar and he will do just what he promised.

When I was in my third year of salvation, I wanted a husband so bad. It was a young guy that kept telling me I was his wife. I started to believe him because I was tired of waiting. Then it was another guy that I thought was my husband. He was handsome and close to my age, I knew he must have been the one. He wasn't even saved and plus he was in a relationship. However, I had a dream one night that we were on a train to Heaven and this guy was on this train. I assumed by this dream he was going to be saved really soon and he would be my husband. Still today I believe that he will one day surrender his life to Christ however, he was not my husband. I was so tangled up. The devil had captivated my mind. I would visualize marrying the young guy then a few hours later I will picture myself being married to the other guy. I couldn't sleep because my mind stayed on the both of them constantly and I felt I would have to choose one. Then not to mention the other guys that would come into the church that my fellow sisters and brothers in Christ often married me off too. God is not the author of confusion. Don't be fooled by the enemy. When God send someone for you it will be absolute. You will know the truth. His sheep knows his voice and they won't follow any other.

I begin to revert back to childhood games like Mash in my mind. In this paper game, we would list guys on a chart, list your type of houses and the number of children we wanted. Then we did a number rotation eliminating certain things until you came to the final name, house, and number on the chart. The final person was the one you would marry. The final house would be where you would live; the number would determine how many children you would have. I found myself in the middle of Mash; a mental game was going on in my head. I planned my wedding with each of the guys and even considered how our children would look. I had it bad and I was tangled, twisted, and confused. The only way I was able to get out of that tangle was through fasting and praying. I also had my leaders of my church praying with me. I went on a 3 day fast. By the third day that burden had lifted and I felt so free. I deleted numbers, stopped having causal talks with them for months. I wanted them totally out of my system. If you are bound by something or someone it is time to be set free. Remember some things come out only by fasting and praying. Turn your plate down for a few days, seek Gods face and pray. Then separate yourself. God said if my people who are called by my name will humble themselves and pray, and seek my face and turn from their wicked ways; then will I hear from heaven, and will forgive their sin and will heal their land (2 Chronicles 7:14). God heard my prayers, he forgave me for my sins (lusting), and he healed me. He gave me the ability to wait patiently on him. From that moment on I gave myself to Christ and I decided to wait. Every time that spirit of impatience would try to creep in, the Holy Spirit allowed me to see it for what it really was and cast it out. He will do the same for you.

There were other instances where I found myself telling God, God this situation is getting hard. I need you to give me patience and give me a reason to want to wait. I learned that when I asked for patience, my patience was tested. I'm impatient in things that I sometime overlook because I think they are small. I am an impatient driver. I do not like being behind slow driving cars especially if I am in a hurry. Sometimes, I get impatient with my love ones. There are times I get impatient with people at work. Then I begin to question God. Why should I wait for things to change around? The answer is why not wait?

Waiting for God's timing is important. God time is not our time. To everything there is a season, a time for every purpose under heaven." (NKJV). Ecc 3:1. I believe that God has a mate for you and it's not your season yet. God is pruning you to be the person he needs you to be for him and he is pruning your mate to be the person he need for you. If God prematurely blesses you with the things that you ask for, those blessings can over take you and possibly lead you away from God.

When I look at the word wait, it is a verb and it can be defined as a state of pose or to remain inactive until something expected happens. When we have been praying and we believe God for a certain thing we have to remain inactive because we are in expectancy of God. Don't move ahead of God. Don't make a plan B when you are believing God for plan A. Stand still and see the salvation of the Lord

In the mist of our waiting, we want to wait in the right attitude. The right mental attitude is what causes us to wait in peace. When you are waiting you have to know how to handle being single. Single living has its ups and downs and can be hard if you allow it to be. Dealing with singleness takes a mind alteration; the renewing of the mind. The children of Israel had a hard time dealing with the reality they had been delivered from slavery. Although they had physically made a transition they hadn't quite made the spiritual transition in their hearts and minds. There is a transition in your spirit that has to take place during the wait; especially if you have or had a mentality that revolves around a companion. The children of Israel had a slave mentality. There are many women and men that think that if a man or woman is not in their lives then the world is against them. This is a slave mentality to man's validation. This mentality will have you disobedient to your parents, cause you to neglect your children, and disown friends. Especially if that's what it takes to keep that man in your life.

I once had an associate every time she got into a relationship she would stop all communications with her friends. We knew when the relationship was over because she would start back calling and coming around. Good thing she didn't have any children at that time; not for sure how that relationship would have ended up. Being single was a very hard position for her. She hated to be alone. She would cry and be down when she was lonely. Depression would have its way with her up until her next relationship. Men were like a bad drug to her; high today and looking for the next hit tomorrow. She was a very pretty young lady. However, she needed a man to fulfill her. She just couldn't seem to wait on God. If your desires for a mate are anything like her, living a saved and single life may be a little difficult for you but you can make it. You may have experienced a lifestyle of inconsistent relationships; one boyfriend after another. When you are tired of going in circles in a relationship, you then learn to wait on God.

Waiting will be difficult for you if you have not given in to Christ totally. There are many steps that people go through to get off drugs and alcohol, but many never complete the first step which is accepting Christ. Unfortunately without Christ many slip right back into bondage. The only secure relationship in life is that which is with Jesus Christ. If you have accepted Christ as he was offered in the previous chapter then it is safe to go on, but be sure not to slip back into bondage.

Coping means to deal with, make out, and come to term with. Coping basically means to have a new way of thinking, a renewed mind. You have to admit to yourself that you are single. You have to admit to yourself that you are saved and that you desire to live right before God. Admitting and acceptance are great steps to success. There are many joys of being single, but at first even I found it to be difficult. I was saved, single, and a single parent. Thoughts and feelings always bombarded my mind. Sometimes confusion and frustration set in. Thoughts of insecurity, lack of time, loneliness, guilt and sexual issues all began to speak to me. I would mediate on those thoughts (big mistake) and I would find myself depressed and oppressed. Don't meditate on things that's against God's order and will. The enemy will play a full movie in your mind. Before you know it you will be ready to act on those thoughts. You have to avoid thoughts that aren't like Christ. If it doesn't line up scripturally, it brings enmity with God; cast down those imaginations.

> "Casting down imaginations, and every high thing that exalteth itself against the knowledge of God, and bringing into captivity every thought to the obedience of Christ; And having in a readiness to revenge all disobedience, when your obedience is fulfilled" (2 Cor 10:5-6).

Speak the word over yourself. It took me a while to get to this place as a single person but I thank God for continuing on and placing me in a hearing position to receive. Feed your spirit with God's word, pray, and avoid watching too much television, social media, and negativity. If you want to be kept God will surely keep you.

The spirit of lack always seemed to creep in. Lack of time, lack of money, lack of companionship controlled my mind. I felt there wasn't enough time in a day to do what I needed to do. No time for myself, no time for my son, and no time to complete tasks. I felt I was young and all I did was go to church and work. I desire more activities in my young age. I felt like my biological clock was ticking and I need to have more children. I felt I needed to complete more. Then God asked me one day what is my rush? He told me that I am on a temporary assignment here on earth. The only task I should be concerned about completing is the one from him, so I can hear the words "Well done my good and faithful servant". We have a habit of looking at what we don't have verses what we do have. Don't rush the process of God. This is a learning stage. So I prayed and prayed and kept praying that God would help me to wait on him. I began to notice a change in my mind and my body began to slow down. I still desired some of those things but I was able to put them in the right prospective and say Lord if it is your will and I only wanted it in God's timing. I was careful not to get into a spirit of apathy but I understood that if it is not in God's will then it is not important. He began to teach me the importance of prioritizing and organization. A life out of order will always conflict with time.

Then there was a lack of security. I felt I worked hard for my money and it was gone as soon as my check hit my account. My funds were being disbursed to everybody except myself. Being a single parent came twice as many bills. I felt I need a man with extra money so he could help out financially. I didn't understand why I never had money. God taught me through his word and the revelation of others the power of money management as well as depending on him. He explained to me that he was my source and the job he blessed me with is my resource. He is Jehovah Jireh he is my provider. God also taught me the art of tithing.

> Bring ye all the tithes into the storehouse, that there may be meat in mine house, and prove me now herewith, saith the LORD of hosts, if I will not open you the windows of heaven, and pour you out a blessing, that there shall not be room enough to receive it (Malachi 3:10).

The secret to being blessed is to give. You have to be a good steward over that which God has blessed you with. No matter how many bills come my way, no matter what my credit score maybe, and no matter how much money is in my bank account. He is a provider and he will supply my needs. I'm not saying that I never have financial difficulties because I do, but I am a dependent of the Most High. So I stand on the fact that my parent is God and he will not lie. Depend totally on your Father God. You are a King's kid.

> God is not a man that he should lie; neither the son of man that he should repent: hath he said, and

shall he not do it? or hath he spoken, and shall he not make it good? (**Numbers 23:19**).

You have to have the same mindset. God has the power and the ability to do whatever he will. Don't fret the small things. Money is a small thing. Having a companion is a small thing and sometimes a bigger headache. Things of the spirit are big things.

There are different demons and spirits that look for bodies to house themselves. The bible tells us that the devil is like a roaring lion seeking whom he may devour. The spirit of loneliness is a very familiar spirit that lingers around singles. Be careful because this spirit will attach itself to you like leeches. I lived in a state of loneliness. I learned that loneliness is an emotional mindset. When there is a lack of the presence of someone then your mind begins to tell your body that it's lonely. The body will tell the mind that you are bored and you need someone around to have fun. When this spirit comes upon you, you have to speak to it. Throughout the Bible God told me that he will not leave me, nor will he forsake me. Forsake means "give up". God told me that he will never leave me nor will he give up on me. He told me that he dwells in me. The fullness of the God head completes me. Therefore I am never alone. "I am not lonely because Jesus lives on the inside. If God lives in you then you are never alone either. I realized that if anything, I should be saying I am not alone I do not need company because I have "The company keeper" living on the inside.

The spirit of guilt is another spirit that would overshadow me. This is just one example. When my son was misbehaving in school, acting ungodly, and acting like he had no home training; I allowed the enemy to condemn me of being a bad parent. I let guilt set in because I felt if I hadn't been living in sin then my son's father would be in his life. I took his behavior as an act of disappointment for his father not being present. I blamed myself for this separation, for my son attitude, and his behavior. Many nights I would lie in bed thinking how I could fix this situation. I was living right at least I thought I was and I just didn't understand. God reminded me one night that the devil is a lie. You are living right and he told me that there is no condemnation for those that are in Christ Jesus. I am in Christ. The devil will bring all types of lies to you when you are going through. Don't react. The plan of satan was for me to never reach my destiny that had been pre-ordained by God. The devil couldn't seem to make me fall so he attacked me through my son. If he can't reach you directly he will use someone else to get to you. He began to work on the one that was the closest earthly person to me; my son. It got so bad at one point I even thought about moving back home and making it work with my son's father, just to make him happy. There were times I would even call my son's father and beg for the relationship to be mended for our son's sake. I had come to a point where I was willing to sacrifice my happiness, my joy, and my salvation for my son's happiness. Don't allow the love of others to supersede your love for God. Don't allow guilt to move you out of God. I prayed and nothing seemed to get better. I fasted and things sometimes seemed to get worst. I went to leadership in church and they prayed for me. God knows how to speak in the midst of the storm. He spoke and said, "cast your cares on me for I care you" then he said, "forgetting those things which are

behind, and reaching forth unto those things which are
before, press toward the mark for the prize of the high
calling of God in Christ Jesus." After hearing these words I
decided to press on in spite of this situation. I gave my son
to God and I let it go. Don't go back to your past. Keep
moving forward. After I let go and gave him and the
situation to the Lord it still seemed worst but I kept praying
and I kept fasting. I prayed for him and sometimes I cried
but I still believed God. I remember after the storm, my
Pastor walked over to me and said, "Praise God you made
it through. I was praying for you". It feels good to know
that others are praying for you. In order to keep your walk
pure we have to let things and people go. Stick close to
those that can help you on your spiritual journey. We can't
bring people from our past into our future that is not
supposed to be there. Don't allow your past to distract you.
Tune out the distracting and tune in to God's station. God
said to cast your cares upon him. Even if it is your children
give them to God. He is the parent of all parents so he
knows how to take better care of them then any of us.

Sexual issues and hormone tried to terminate my walk
with God by the lust of the eye, lust of the flesh, and pride
of life. When the hormones kicked in the flesh began to
send signals to the mind that told me to go get what I
wanted and act however I chose to, but I thank God for
Jesus. If I would have obeyed my flesh I probably would
have picked up some spirits and diseases that I could not
get rid of. The flesh is at enmity to God (Romans 8:7). I
truly thank God I was able to stand my ground and it is a
continuing stand.

The most mind blowing spirit was the spirit of doubt. I
know there are many that have been single longer than I.

However in those years, the days and weeks begin to get long. The enemy would bring me thoughts that I would be by myself for the rest of my life and I would die lonely. I began to believe his lies for a moment because how long it was taking. God has a time for us. We have to rest in his presence and know that he is moving accordingly. Don't allow the enemy to bring you false hopes. Speak those things that be not as though they were. My husband is here.

My mind and my flesh always wanted me to fulfill every thought, idea, and suggestion that came to mind. However, I learned a mind without Christ is a mind set and ready for destruction. This is why we as Christians have to get understanding. Lean to live in whatever position the Lord has you in. Overcoming thoughts that the enemy bring to you allow you to deal with single living. We have to allow God to renew our minds daily. "God said pick up my cross and walk with me daily"···This is part of the mind renewing process. These are just some of the issues that you may face.

Pray this prayer:

God help me to wait. Help me to wait with the right attitude and with the right intentions. Let your will and timing take full effect in my life. When I seem to get impatient calm my spirit and give me to wait on you Lord. Knowing that if I wait on you, you will renew my strength, I shall run and not be weary; I shall mount up with wings like Eagles, I shall walk and not faint. Lord help me not to allow my situation and circumstances to turn me away from you. Help me to have a made up mind. Lord

reveal your love to me so I will not stray. Lord give
me the wisdom to understand it. In Jesus Nam!
Amen!

Chapter 8

Don't Allow Temptation To Make You Backslid

Temptation is a test or trial that is designed to make you or
break you. The book of James tells us that temptation is the
testing of our faith. We should "count it all joy when ye fall
into divers temptations, knowing that the trying of our faith
worketh patience" (James 1:2-3). Webster's Dictionary
defines temptation as an act that looks appealing to an
individual. As I begin to study, I found that the word
temptation is found 21 times in the New Testament. The
Greek word for temptation is "Peirasmos". Peirasmos
means to be tested or tried by troubles, conflict,
confrontation, and/or persecution. Trials are meant to be
endured but temptations should be avoided.   In order to
fully understand a peirasmos you have to have discernment.
Remember that satan's tactics are the "lust of the eye, lust
of the flesh, and pride of life" (1 John2:16). Temptation is
the enticing to do wrong. Therefore we can look at
temptation as a growth enhancer or a friend to failure.
Being tempted is normal. Everyone has and will be tempted

to do something they shouldn't do. No one is exempt from temptations. We are blessed when we endure temptation. God has promised us the crown of life. Temptation is not a sin; it is the yielding to the temptation that causes sin and sin brings about death. God does not bring temptation it comes from Satan. In the Garden of Eden, God had given Adam specific instructions. He said you can eat from every tree of the garden but not from the tree of knowledge of good and evil. For in that day if you eat from this tree you will surely die. I imagine that Adam and Eve were in the garden doing whatever it was they did and minding their own business and suddenly satan crept in to Eve. Eve was tempted by a serpent, which was satan. She was the first to rebel against God by being disobedient. The fruit was shared with Adam and immediately there was a separation that took place when he chose to eat of the fruit. Their eyes were opened, they knew they were naked, and they were fearful. Spiritual and physical death came into the world and our fellowship with God was broken. When you act or participate in the temptation (sin) immediately our fellowship with God is broken. Thank God for our perfect Lamb, Jesus that came to correct the wrong. You do not want to be disconnected from our source of life.

Jesus was the perfect example of how to overcome temptation. Jesus was in the wilderness where he had been fasting for forty days and forty nights. The bible says that Jesus was hungry. Can you imagine going 40 days without eating? I believe that Jesus was really hungry. So of course satan always come when you are at your weakest point. He came to Jesus and tempted him three times. Satan was determined to get Jesus to turn against God. With every strategy that satan brought to Jesus, Jesus had a great come back. You can only fight satan with the word of God; for it is written. Satan knows the word of God as well. He came to Jesus, Adam, and Eve with the word of God. This is why it is important that you know the word of God inside out, through and through, from Genesis to Revelation. Read, meditate, and study the word of God daily. Make it your lifestyle. Continue to resist the devil. He will leave but believe me he will come again at a more opportune time.

I encountered a situation a few years ago. I was working as a loan officer, and I recall the time I had a member that I approved and finalized an auto loan for. He was so excited because I helped him to obtain his dream car. After the closing, I found an envelope on my desk and inside was $360.00. I immediately got happy because my lights had just got cut off the day before and my bill was $356.00 to get them back on. I just knew that this was a blessing from God. However, the Holy Spirit began to convict me. It was wrong to accept that money on many levels. You may think immediately that was a blessing, just like I. Satan knows our needs and desires. So he will come in during that time to kill, steal, and destroy. This is why it is very import to be wise and not foolish. Previously the customer asked me out, his ex-girlfriend was working with me, and policy at work is we cannot receive any monetary gifts from customers. I had to give it back. He refused to receive it back so I deposited it in his account. This is an example of discerning a temptation and a blessing. I was tempted to keep the money and get my lights cut back on. However, if I would have taken that gift he would have expected something in return. My father always told me to be careful accepting things from men because eventually they will want something in return. Not only that, if it would have gotten back to my employer I would have gotten fired. And of course it would have caused a big confrontation with his ex-girlfriend which was my co-worker. God always has a ram in the bush. The next day I got an unexpected bonus on my check. I was able to get my lights back on after all. Never settle when you are expecting more from God.

We have to learn to resist the devil. James tells us in 4:7, 'to resist the devil and he will flee from us." However, He also says that we must submit ourselves to God. In the submission to God, the flesh begins to die out. It is easier to overcome temptation when the Holy Spirit is our guidance. It is God that makes us strong enough to resist the devil. If you miss communion with God, studying your word, forsaking the assembling with your brethren, then you will be weak and it will be harder to resist the devil. You will find yourself falling for satan's strategies. Draw near to him so you may be able to stand the wiles of the enemy.

If you ever wondered why it's not working when you say, "Go devil or lose your hold," it's probably because you're not close enough to God. Even when you say those things, the torment and the harassment of the enemy may continue but you will be able to resist the temptations.

Satan will make sin attractive and make you think you are missing out on something. Do not allow the enemy to cause you to turn back due to temptation. The enemy desire is to make us lose our faith in God and turn away from him. Don't go back to where God has delivered you from. Backsliding is easy if you're not careful. Remember the enemy is subtle and he will attack whomever. It doesn't matter who you are, what's your title, or how much money you have. It has no sympathy and no picks and chooses. You can be sitting in the church on the front pew and be in a backslidden position. A rebellious spirit can cause you to backslide. Disobedience can cause you to backslide. Lack of faith and lack of time with God can cause you to backslide.

When I first got saved I was under a ministry that did not allow us to have a boyfriend or girlfriend. There was no dating or courting allowed. I thought this was the craziest thing someone could ever say. Having been in church all of my life, I had never been told that I couldn't have a boyfriend and wait on God to bring me a husband. In the world, I was always told to date first and get to know their family before you marry a person so you could know who you are marrying. The churches I attended in the past made it seem like it was ok to go out and do your thing all week as long as you were in church Sunday morning. So I did just that. I was a sinner that did my due diligence of going to church. I was simply a church going sinner on my way to HELL. It was hard to wrap the fact of no boyfriend in Christ around my mind. I always dreamed of finding my knight in shining armor, dating, and falling in love. I wanted that love that was portrayed on television. I wanted my life to go my way. Though my way and my thinking is what caused my chaotic past but it didn't matter to me. I was used to serving God one way and I did not want to adjust. Although, my salvation experience this time was different, I was set on having it my way. I had experienced God on a level like never before, but I still wanted to bring my religious traditions into this new walk.

Being a new baby in Christ I did not have a full understanding of Christianity. I had been in church all my life, I never really paid attention. So I was rebellious against the truth of there is no boyfriends and girlfriends in Christ. My Pastor would always say, "I have read 32 translations of the Holy Bible and not one of them say anything about boyfriends and girlfriends. I have only read husbands and wives." Regardless of what he would say I would still say you can't get a husband without first having a boyfriend. Because of my lack of understanding and my rebellious stage I backslid seeking a boyfriend. I never fornicated but I came really close. I had backslid in my mind. Backsliding always take place in the mind first. If the enemy can seize your mind then he can cause you to do anything. This is why the helmet of salvation is so much needed. The enemy first gets you with the lust of eye. And this is exactly what he was doing to me.

I went back south to visit for the holidays. I had an ex-boyfriend I hadn't seen in months that mysteriously popped up at my parents' house because he heard I was in town. When I saw him I thought he was fine and the cutest person I had ever seen. He wasn't even fine and cute when we were dating, but this was the trick of the enemy. He makes things seem better than what they are. Old feelings begin to come up and past memories. The lust of the eye and the lust of the flesh led me to want to be alone with him. He asked if we could hang out later. Of course I was eager to say yes. Starting with a late night movie and later too his home. We were only talking but my flesh wanted more than just a conversation. Touching and feeling was not a part of the plan that night but it became the plan for the both of us. In the heat of the moment I felt God presence remove from me. Although we did not sleep together it was close enough for God to grab my attention. At that time I knew the ideology of not having a boyfriend. I was scared and all I could say was "Lord I'm sorry please forgive me". The guy began to lash out saying that I was a teaser and a flirt, but I thank God for his protection. I could have been raped or killed. There were so many emotions I was feeling that night. I felt afraid, nervous, yucky, sick, low, sad, guilty, and ashamed. I was scared to go back to my parents' house because they knew I was saved. My sister is also saved and she has the gift of discernment and the gift of prophecy and they are always in operation. I knew she would know as soon as I walked in. I also had to go back home to church. My Pastor had a gift where he can look you in your face and tell you your whole life story. He knew when we had done wrong. I was scared. Nevertheless, if anyone knew of this incident then it was never brought to my attention. Thank God. I was already feeling guilty and I didn't think at that time I could handle other people knowing. This is a place that you should never have to visit. If you have been here, you should never want to go back.

I learned that when there are feelings involved with someone it is so easy to engage in ungodly acts especially when you are single and lonely. When you have been sexual active your body craves those sexual pleasures and you will be tempted. The enemy always tries to make sin appealing. But God has made a way of escape. Look for the EXIT. Lust will take us out of God and can be dangerous,

Sometimes we have to learn the hard way because that's what we as human choose to do. However, taking the way of God will be easy.

Begin to bathe your hormones in prayer. God has the power to change any and everything. Pray, God take every sexual desire from you until the appointed time. It works because I am a living witness. I began to pray that prayer fervently after my 2nd year of salvation. I noticed how those feelings rarely came until they were suddenly gone.

I once heard one of the sisters in the church say how she prayed when she was single. She prayed for herself and she prayed for her husband. She said, "go to God for yourself and be real. Let him know your struggles. He is aware of them anyway but admitting it to yourself, helps you to realize that you have a problem and need God's help". Ask God to take away every sexual desire and even ask him to erase past memories. Ask him to renew you. Ask him to give your sexual desires back at the appointed time (when you are married).

Pray this prayer:

Father I come to you in the name of Jesus help me Lord to overcome every temptation. Lord help me not to fall into the traps of Satan. Every evil and vain thought that comes help me Lord to bring it into captivity to the obedience of Christ. Open my eyes Lord so I may see clearly. God help me not to fail in the midst of my trails. Lord be with me and guide me. Help me to learn and pass every test. Lord don't allow me to backslide or lose focus. Help me to keep Jesus at the center of my attention, In Jesus Name, Amen.

Chapter 9

Purpose

Are you dissatisfied? Do you feel like you are constantly going in circles? Do you question yourself, why am I here? Do you wonder why you were created? Do you feel like the black sheep in the family? Do you feel that you do not fit in? These are some questions I used to often ask myself. These questions can only be answered once you understand your purpose; the plan of God for your life.

Ask the Lord, God what is my purpose? Why are you so mindful of me that you allow me to continue on living in this land? Whether your questions have been answered or not, know that you have a reason for living. We are all on this earth for a purpose. Your purpose is not just to be in a marriage and have children. Your purpose is not just to have a successful career and make a good living. Though that is a nice position to have and many of us dream about living life with access to tangible and intangible resources, but God's purpose is far greater. The family, jobs, and money is just added benefits. Purpose is the reason something is done or created. It is the reason something exists. Our purpose for living was established by our Creator. God is the only one that can give us a clear insight to why we were created. Don't look to man for your purpose. God's purpose for each of our lives is to have fellowship with him and give him praise. We were created by our creator for our creator to give him Glory.

> "Even every one that is called by my name: for I
> have created him for my glory, I have formed him;
> yea, I have made him. "(Is. 43:7)

Your purpose for living is to ultimately give God glory through praise and worship. We give God praise and worship with our lives. This is done by the way we live our lives. God in his awesome wisdom and love planned for us this perfect life according to his will before we were ever born or even formed in our mother's womb. Jesus came so we could have an abundant life.

> "The thief comes to kill, steal, and destroy but Jesus
> came so that we may have life and have life more
> abundantly". (John 10:10)

To fully understand your purpose you must first understand the life God has given unto us. Life is not just the means of existing. There are many people who are merely existing but not living. Some issues that have occurred in your life may have caused your purpose to be foggy and now you merely exist. "Zoe" is the Greek word for life; God's quality of life, everlasting life. This is the type of life that Jesus talks about in the book of St John.

This life is only received through the rebirth. For this reason, salvation is the foundation of living. That is first and the most important step of your life. In order to receive what God has for you, you must stop existing and start living. Stop allowing Satan's attacks to kill, steal, and destroy your viewpoint of your life purpose.

Understand that the things you have endured and are going to endure is simply a process to promote you to your purpose. People may have hurt you, talked about you, misused you, and may have lied on you. Those pains, those scars, and those wounds are designed for your purpose. God was molding you in every bad and good situation for your purpose. Don't allow your past to harden your heart. Don't allow hurt to cripple you. Don't allow fear to stagnant you. Fear is false evidence appearing real. Fear will keep you from your purpose. It will handicap your life and keep you in disparity in this world. You have a purpose to fulfill and a destiny to reach. So keep pressing in for God and don't take your eyes off the prize which is Jesus.

What God has called you to do, do it. It is a part of your process to your purpose. Failure to launch out when God has given you something to do can be a danger to your purpose. When God tells us to do something it is for our good. Move accordingly.

> "For I know the thoughts that I think toward you, saith the LORD, thoughts of peace, and not of evil, to give you an expected end. (Jer. 29:11).

Our expected end in life is to make Heaven our home.

Heaven is our destiny. How do you make Heaven your home? By fulfilling your God given purpose and by living a life that is pleasing to our creator. God has already prepared a place. We just have to follow the blueprint.

> "Let not your heart be troubled: ye believe in God, believe also in me. In my Father's house are many mansions: if it were not so, I would have told you. I go to prepare a place for you. And if I go and prepare a place for you, I will come again, and receive you unto myself; that where I am, there ye may be also. And whither I go ye know, and the way ye know. (John 14:1-4)"

Don't be concerned about what you have going on in your life. Don't allow discouragement to sit in because what you see happening around you. Make sure that when things are going great that you do not forget about your purpose. Remember when things are going wrong keep your purpose in mind; and walk in your purpose no matter how you feel or what it looks like. After the death of Jesus, the disciples went back to doing what they were doing before they were called by Him; which was fishing. Their Master had transition and apparently they assumed their purpose was over or either they chose not to continue on their purpose journey. Jesus had to step onshore just to remind them what they had been called to do. Jesus is doing the same now. He is saying don't lose focus and don't go back to doing what you were doing before. A spouse and children are not your purpose. They may be a part of the process to produce your purpose but it's not the ultimate call of God for you.

In fulfilling your purpose, watch the company you keep. Some people you are associated with are dream killers and they will keep you from your purpose. You will find yourself not keeping God's commandment but keeping the commandment of people that don't have any meaning in your life. You have to know your purpose so when people like these surround you; you will have a plan of action to dissimilate yourself. When you don't know or understand your purpose you will be wondering in life with the wrong people. You will have no peace, no joy, and no contentment. You are called to give God glory, praise, and worship and to be a servant of our Lord. Go fulfill your purpose.

Pray this prayer:

Father I know that you know the plans for my life. I know that your ways are not my ways and Lord I understand that I have a purpose for living. I know that my purpose it to worship you in spirit and in truth with my whole life. God I know that it is my job to know you for myself and to have an on fire relationship with you. God give me to wisdom and knowledge to fully understand what is required of me and the reason I was created. God I appreciate you in my life and I appreciate you for giving me life more abundantly. Thank you for your grace and your mercies. Help me to get to the place that nothing and nobody else matters. Help me to live my life according to your will so that I may be walking in my purpose. Help me to fully understand my purpose and to fulfill your plan. God, every gift and talent you have given unto me help me to use it for your glory and to edify the body of Christ. As I face challenges in my life help me to always look to Jesus. Even when everything seems to be working in my favor, Lord help me to look to you. Help me to reflect my purpose in my day to day activities. In Jesus Name. Amen!

Conclusion

If you adhere to the pre-requisites in this book, you have what it takes to make it as a saved, sanctified, single person of God. You have been engrafted, meaning you have been made one with Christ. This does not mean that we are God. If you listen and yield to the Spirit of God, this walk will be a smooth sail. God has called you to be single and he has called you to a higher level. Many are called but few are chosen. Accept being Gods' chosen one. We tend to get excited about the wrong things in life. You get excited when we are chosen for a promotion at work or chosen to be the speaker at an event so you have to be excited to be chosen by God to be single.

Be careful of the position you so much desire. It may not be the position for you at this time. Be content where God has you and learn to wait on the Lord. It shouldn't matter what position we are chosen for by God. All positions in God are exciting and great positions.

I'm reminded of a story in the book of Matthew, the sons of Zebedee. James and John were called to be disciples of Jesus Christ, which is a great position. Their mothers came to Jesus and began to worship him. She desired for her two sons to sit on the right and left hand of

Jesus. Jesus asked, "do you know what you ask?"

Do you understand what you really ask God for?

The revelation of the matter is that being single is a position in Christ. It's a place where you can have uninterrupted communion with God. Don't rush the perfection of Christ. He is doing a work in you. He's molding and making you and preparing you for greatness. Your Boaz is being made perfectly for you. Stand in the process.

> "Therefore, my beloved brethren, be ye stedfast, unmovable, always abounding in the work of the Lord, forasmuch as ye know that your labour is not in vain in the Lord." (Matt:15:58)

Don't get weary in well doing and thinking that your knight and shiny armor will not come. Continue to focus on the things of the Lord. Seek the Kingdom of God first. This will work in your favor.

Accept the person God has for you. We will accept everything else but find faults in things of God. Right before my night and shiny armor appeared. I was in Walmart and this nicely built man was in the aisle. A friend and I were admiring the workmanship of God. He had properly made that young man. My friend and I began to joke and make silly statements letting God know that is what we wanted in a man. There is nothing wrong with praying for certain characteristics in your mate or being specific with God. Yet our desires are not always in the will of God's plan. In this case the Holy Ghost began to convict me. I was lusting after someone that wasn't for me. The Holy Ghost rose up in my spirit and loud and clear I heard God say, "That's the reason I can't give you what you want. You would love him more than you love me". That was conviction and an eye opener. I then begin to say God I will have whoever you have for me because I know it will be your best. You have to get to that position. When you honestly lie before God and surrender it all to him, God will move on your behalf.

Whatever it is you believing God for today lay it at the feet of Jesus and cast all of your cares on him. Now sit back and watch God move for you. Accept the call of being single, appropriate the revelation of waiting and learning to live without a mate and appreciate all that God has done for you. In the midst, build a life of prayer and fasting and meditating on God's word daily. The spiritual exercise will strengthen you. It is substantial for your faith walk. Get into a bible teaching church so that you can begin to grow into the full knowledge and understanding of Christ. Fall in love with yourself. Accept who God has made you.

It is just about every woman's desire to have a wonderful husband and marvelous children. Ask God to begin to prepare you to receive who he has for you. God Bless

Yours Truly

Casey Jackson-Ware

Casey Jackson–Ware

Prayers for Singles:

Father In the name of Jesus,

I come boldly to you being as open as I know how. Lord I lay every issue, worry, doubt, pain, situation, envy, jealousy, strife, unforgiveness, my past, my present, and my future at your feet. I cast all of my cares on you. I ask for forgiveness for all of my sins those known and unknown. Wash me Lord. Purify me Lord. Create in me a clean heart and renew in me a right spirit. Help me to forgive and let it go. Lord let your spirit dwell in me so I may be in right standing with you. As a single woman help me to present my body to you as a living sacrifice, holy, and acceptable. Lord I give myself to you. Help me to accept myself and fall in love with the person you have made me to be. For I am fearfully and wonderfully made. And you have beautified the meek with salvation. Your light shines bright through me and I am a radiant glow. Because of you I am of a high value. You have redeemed me so I count myself to be worthy of all you have for me. I am forgetting those things which are behind. I am forgetting those things that people have spoken about me. God uproot every evil and ugly word that has been spoken over me. I am letting go of people thoughts of me. Lord I love all of me including my imperfections and flaws. I appreciate the person you have made me to be. Help me to walk in confidence knowing that you did not make a mistake with me. I am pressing forward in you. I am a yielded vessel ready to be used by you. As I am on this journey help me to wait patiently for your will to be done in my life. Help me not to attach

myself to the wrong people. Help me not to give up or give
in and settle for less, when I know you have more for me.
While I am standing build me up where I've been torn
down. Restore my faith, my love for you, my joy, my
peace, my self-esteem, and my self-worth. Mold me and
make me to what you want me to be. Prepare me to receive
who you have for me. Help me to get rid of excess baggage
and mend my brokenness. I release the past right now in
the name of Jesus. I pled the blood of Jesus over my
thoughts. Lord I want to be ready to receive all of you as
well as my Boaz. As I wait on you, I pray for the man that
you have designed just for me. I pray that you will mold
and make him. Lord draw him closer to you. God let him
love you with all of his heart, mind, and soul. Lord teach
him how to love me as Christ loves the church. God protect
the suitable man you have for me. Keep him safe in your
arms. Keep his mind stayed on you. Help him to be a good
provider, an exceptional husband and father. Give him to
honor me as his wife and our wedding vows. Help me to
respect him as my husband and be the best helpmate for
him. I ask Lord that you will draw our spirits together
even now before we meet. Lord prepare both of us to
receive one another.

I come against the snares of the enemy that comes to hinder
and hold up this union. I bind every evil work and plan
that may have been assigned to us. I pled the blood of
Jesus. I know that at the name of Jesus demons even
tremble. So we speak Jesus in our relationship. Jesus you be
the glue that will bind us together forever.

In Jesus name I pray,

Amen

Singles Daily Affirmation:

Day 1: God's loves me (John 3:16). I love God (Luke 10:27). God is here with me (Deut. 31:6). God is merciful towards me (Psalms 86:15). I thank God for grace (2 Cor. 12:9). I am a child of God (1 John 3:1).

Day 2: God created me (Genesis 1:26). I am God's workmanship (Eph 2:10).God you formed me and I am fearfully and wonderfully made (Psalms 139:13–14)

Day 3: God has saved me (Psalms 55:16). I have been forgiven (Romans 5:8–1Cor. 15:3). I am free from sin (Col. 2:11). I have been crucified with Christ (Gal 2:20).

Day 4: I thank God for a renewed mind (Romans 12:2). I am a new creation (2 Cor. 5:17). I thank God that I possess the fruit of the Spirit (Gal 5:22)

Day 5: God I will not worry (Mt. 6:34). I trust you Lord (Prov 3:5–6). God is working on my behalf (Romans 8:28).

Day 6: I have strength (Is 40:29–31). I have joy (Neh 8:10). I have peace (Phil. 4:7). I am healed (Jer. 17:14; Is. 53:5). Nothing shall separate me from God (Romans 8:31)

Day 7: I can do all things through Christ that strengthens me (Phil 4:13). Nothing is impossible for God (Luke 18:27). I am more than a conquerors (Romans 8:37).

Singles Prayer Exercise:

1. What challenges are you now facing with being single that are hindering your walk with Jesus?

2. Identify things that you would like for God to change within you?

3. Why is being single such a negative aspect of where you currently are in your life?

4. What baggage are you carrying that could be a

potential issue in your future marriage?

5. Write out where the baggage developed and address them, even if that means addressing specific people.

6. List the traits, morals and values that you would like for your mate to possess.

7. If you are in fight for your life, who would you want to come and save you, Jesus or your Boaz? Why?

Dear Single Me:

(Write something encouraging to your single self)

_____

_____

_____

_____

_____

_____

_____

_____

_____

_____

_____

_____

_____

_____

_____

_____

Reasons for Being Single & Thankful:

1.

2.

3.

4.

5.

6.

7.

Goals While Single:

1.

2.

3.

4.

5.

6.

7.

Things I Need To Resolve Before Marriage:

1.

2.

3.

4.

5.

6.

7.

My Plan For Improving My Relationship With God:

43133038R00071

Made in the USA
Middletown, DE
01 May 2017